farlaine the goblin

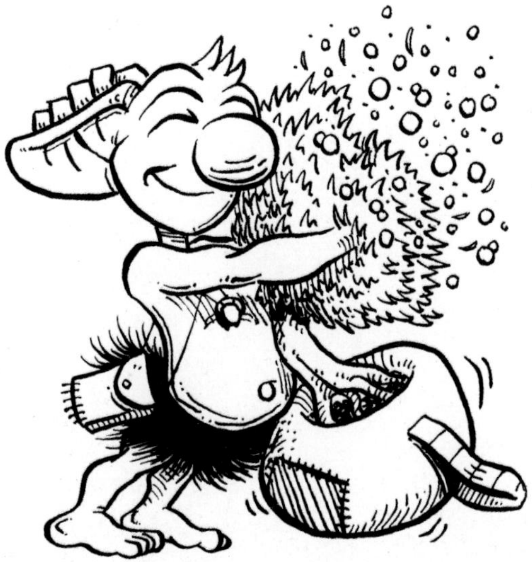

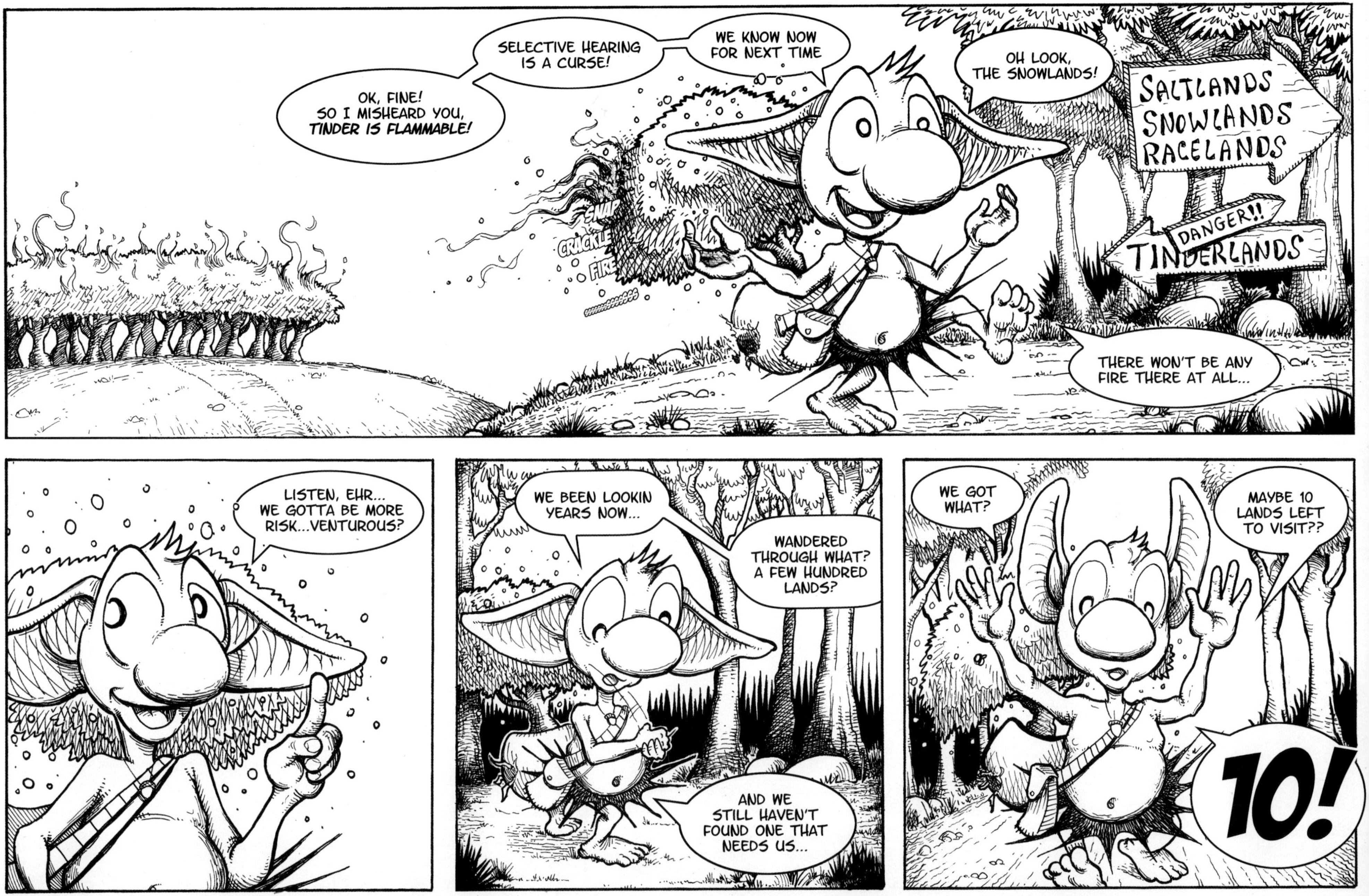
OK, FINE! SO I MISHEARD YOU, *TINDER IS FLAMMABLE!*
SELECTIVE HEARING IS A CURSE!
WE KNOW NOW FOR NEXT TIME
OH LOOK, THE SNOWLANDS!
SALTLANDS SNOWLANDS RACELANDS
DANGER!!
TINDERLANDS
SNAP
CRACKLE
FIRE
THERE WON'T BE ANY FIRE THERE AT ALL...
LISTEN, EHR... WE GOTTA BE MORE RISK...VENTUROUS?
WE BEEN LOOKIN YEARS NOW...
WANDERED THROUGH WHAT? A FEW HUNDRED LANDS?
AND WE STILL HAVEN'T FOUND ONE THAT NEEDS US...
WE GOT WHAT?
MAYBE 10 LANDS LEFT TO VISIT??
10!

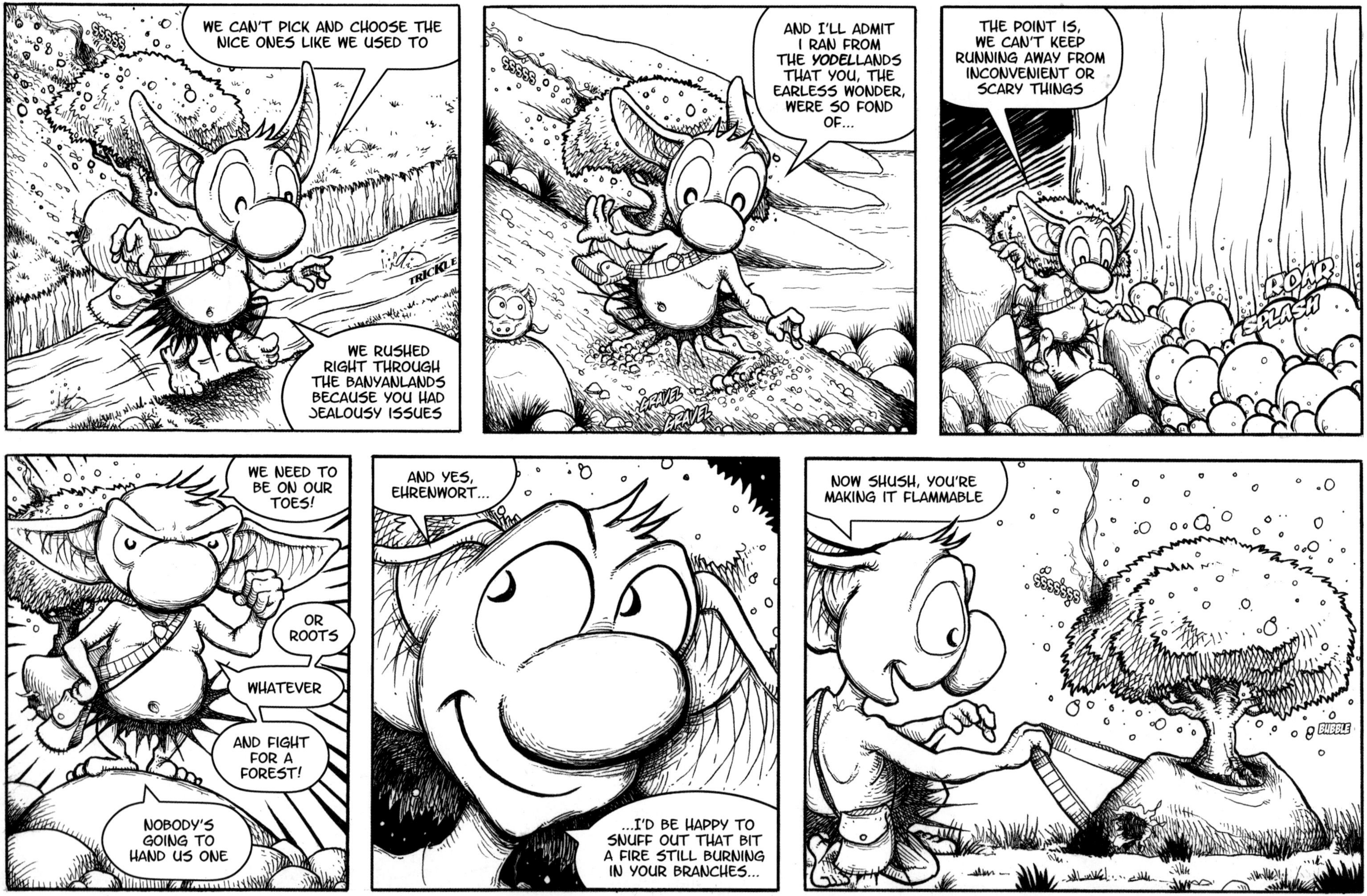
SSSSS
WE CAN'T PICK AND CHOOSE THE NICE ONES LIKE WE USED TO
TRICKLE
WE RUSHED RIGHT THROUGH THE BANYANLANDS BECAUSE YOU HAD JEALOUSY ISSUES
SSSSS
AND I'LL ADMIT I RAN FROM THE YODELLANDS THAT YOU, THE EARLESS WONDER, WERE SO FOND OF...
GRAVEL
GRAVEL
THE POINT IS, WE CAN'T KEEP RUNNING AWAY FROM INCONVENIENT OR SCARY THINGS
ROAR
SPLASH
WE NEED TO BE ON OUR TOES!
OR ROOTS
WHATEVER
AND FIGHT FOR A FOREST!
NOBODY'S GOING TO HAND US ONE
AND YES, EHRENWORT...
...I'D BE HAPPY TO SNUFF OUT THAT BIT A FIRE STILL BURNING IN YOUR BRANCHES...
NOW SHUSH, YOU'RE MAKING IT FLAMMABLE
SSSSSSS
BUBBLE

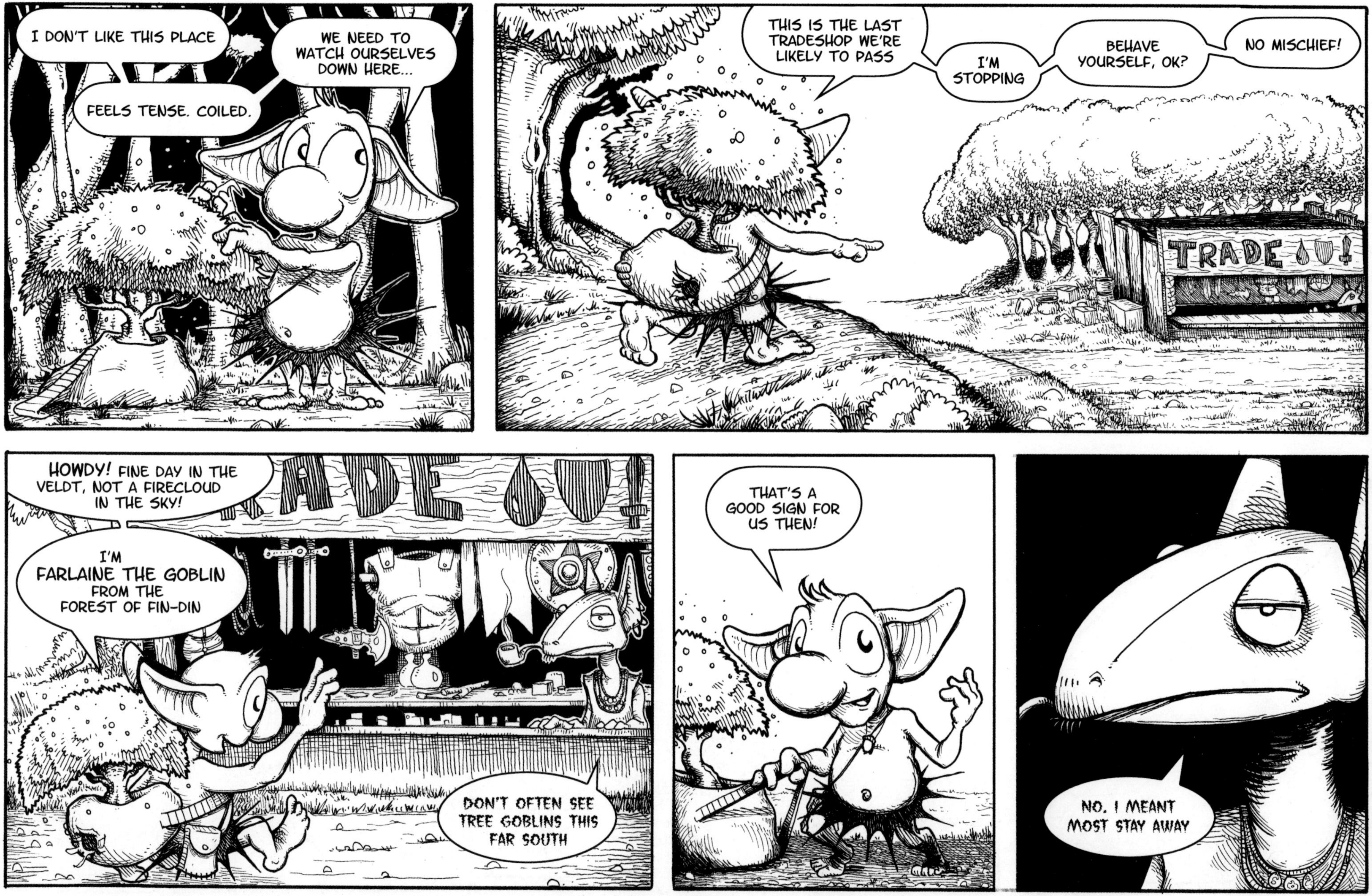
I DON'T LIKE THIS PLACE
FEELS TENSE. COILED.
WE NEED TO WATCH OURSELVES DOWN HERE...
THIS IS THE LAST TRADESHOP WE'RE LIKELY TO PASS
I'M STOPPING
BEHAVE YOURSELF, OK?
NO MISCHIEF!
TRADE
HOWDY! FINE DAY IN THE VELDT, NOT A FIRECLOUD IN THE SKY!
I'M FARLAINE THE GOBLIN FROM THE FOREST OF FIN-DIN
DON'T OFTEN SEE TREE GOBLINS THIS FAR SOUTH
THAT'S A GOOD SIGN FOR US THEN!
NO. I MEANT MOST STAY AWAY

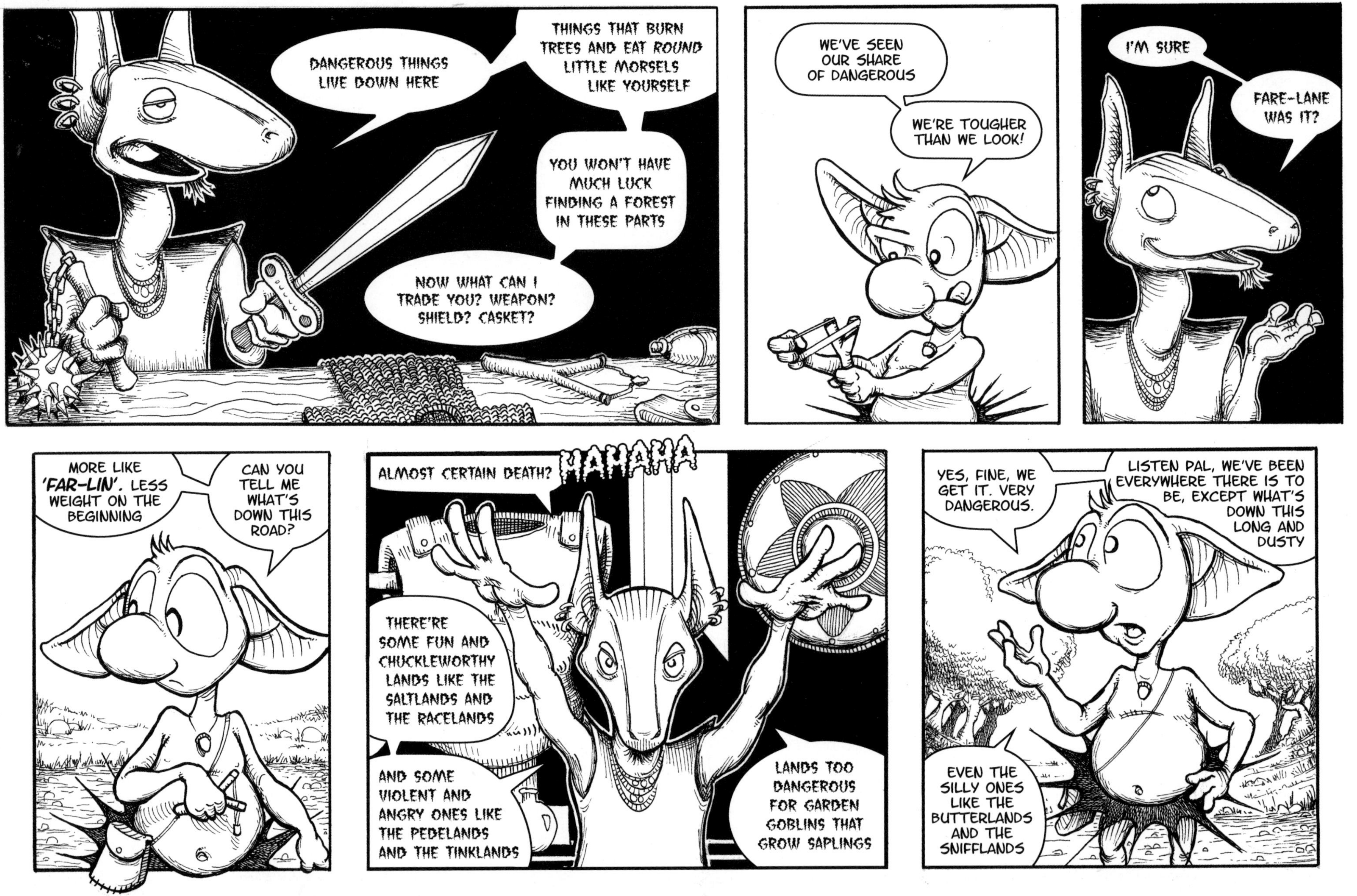
DANGEROUS THINGS LIVE DOWN HERE
THINGS THAT BURN TREES AND EAT *ROUND* LITTLE MORSELS LIKE YOURSELF
YOU WON'T HAVE MUCH LUCK FINDING A FOREST IN THESE PARTS
NOW WHAT CAN I TRADE YOU? WEAPON? SHIELD? CASKET?
WE'VE SEEN OUR SHARE OF DANGEROUS
WE'RE TOUGHER THAN WE LOOK!
I'M SURE
FARE-LANE WAS IT?
MORE LIKE **'FAR-LIN'**. LESS WEIGHT ON THE BEGINNING
CAN YOU TELL ME WHAT'S DOWN THIS ROAD?
ALMOST CERTAIN DEATH?
HAHAHA
THERE'RE SOME FUN AND CHUCKLEWORTHY LANDS LIKE THE SALTLANDS AND THE RACELANDS
AND SOME VIOLENT AND ANGRY ONES LIKE THE PEDELANDS AND THE TINKLANDS
LANDS TOO DANGEROUS FOR GARDEN GOBLINS THAT GROW SAPLINGS
YES, FINE, WE GET IT. VERY DANGEROUS.
LISTEN PAL, WE'VE BEEN EVERYWHERE THERE IS TO BE, EXCEPT WHAT'S DOWN THIS LONG AND DUSTY
EVEN THE SILLY ONES LIKE THE BUTTERLANDS AND THE SNIFFLANDS

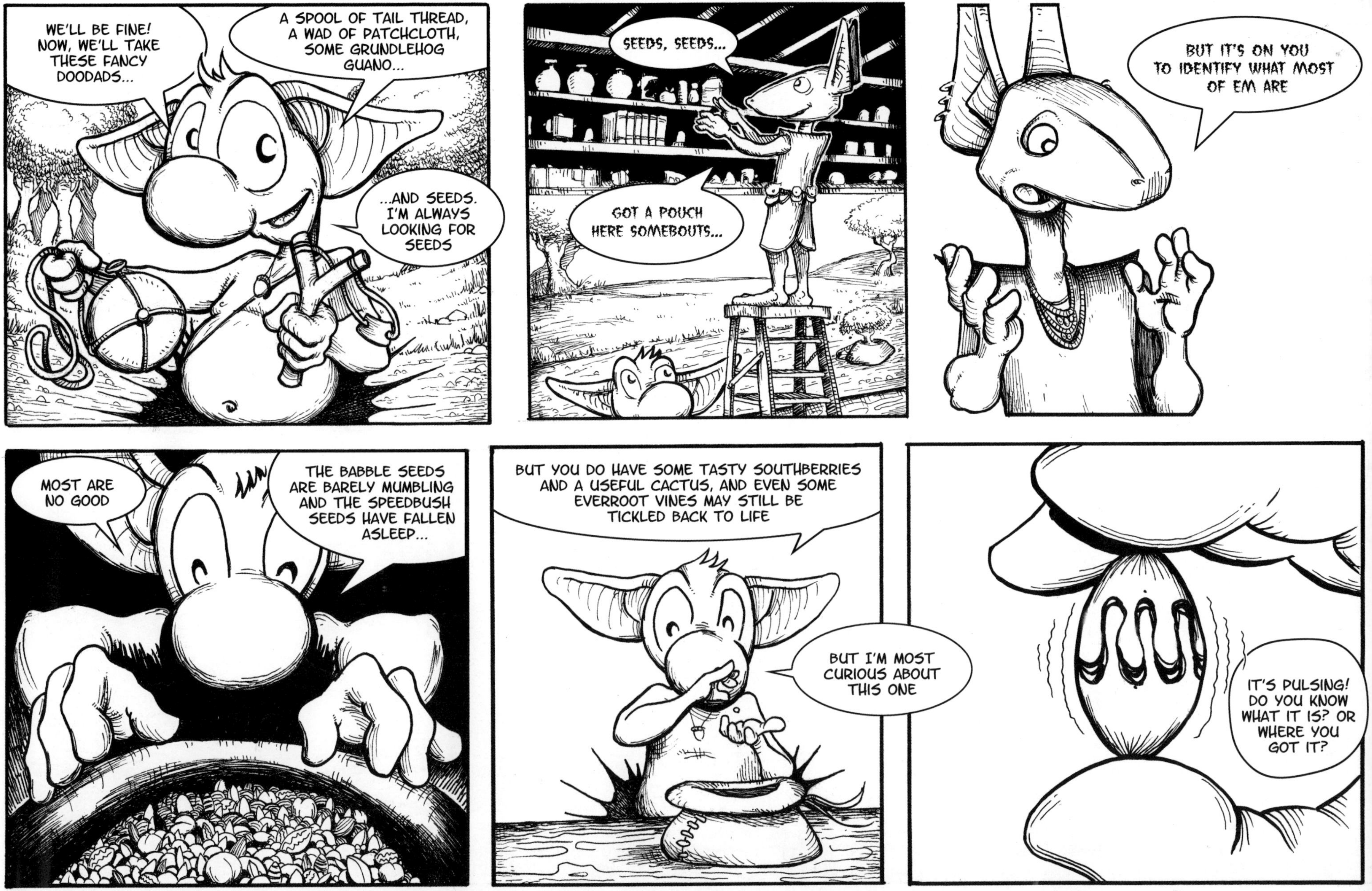
WE'LL BE FINE! NOW, WE'LL TAKE THESE FANCY DOODADS...
A SPOOL OF TAIL THREAD, A WAD OF PATCHCLOTH, SOME GRUNDLEHOG GUANO...
...AND SEEDS. I'M ALWAYS LOOKING FOR SEEDS
SEEDS, SEEDS...
GOT A POUCH HERE SOMEBOUTS...
BUT IT'S ON YOU TO IDENTIFY WHAT MOST OF EM ARE
MOST ARE NO GOOD
THE BABBLE SEEDS ARE BARELY MUMBLING AND THE SPEEDBUSH SEEDS HAVE FALLEN ASLEEP...
BUT YOU DO HAVE SOME TASTY SOUTHBERRIES AND A USEFUL CACTUS, AND EVEN SOME EVERROOT VINES MAY STILL BE TICKLED BACK TO LIFE
BUT I'M MOST CURIOUS ABOUT THIS ONE
IT'S PULSING! DO YOU KNOW WHAT IT IS? OR WHERE YOU GOT IT?

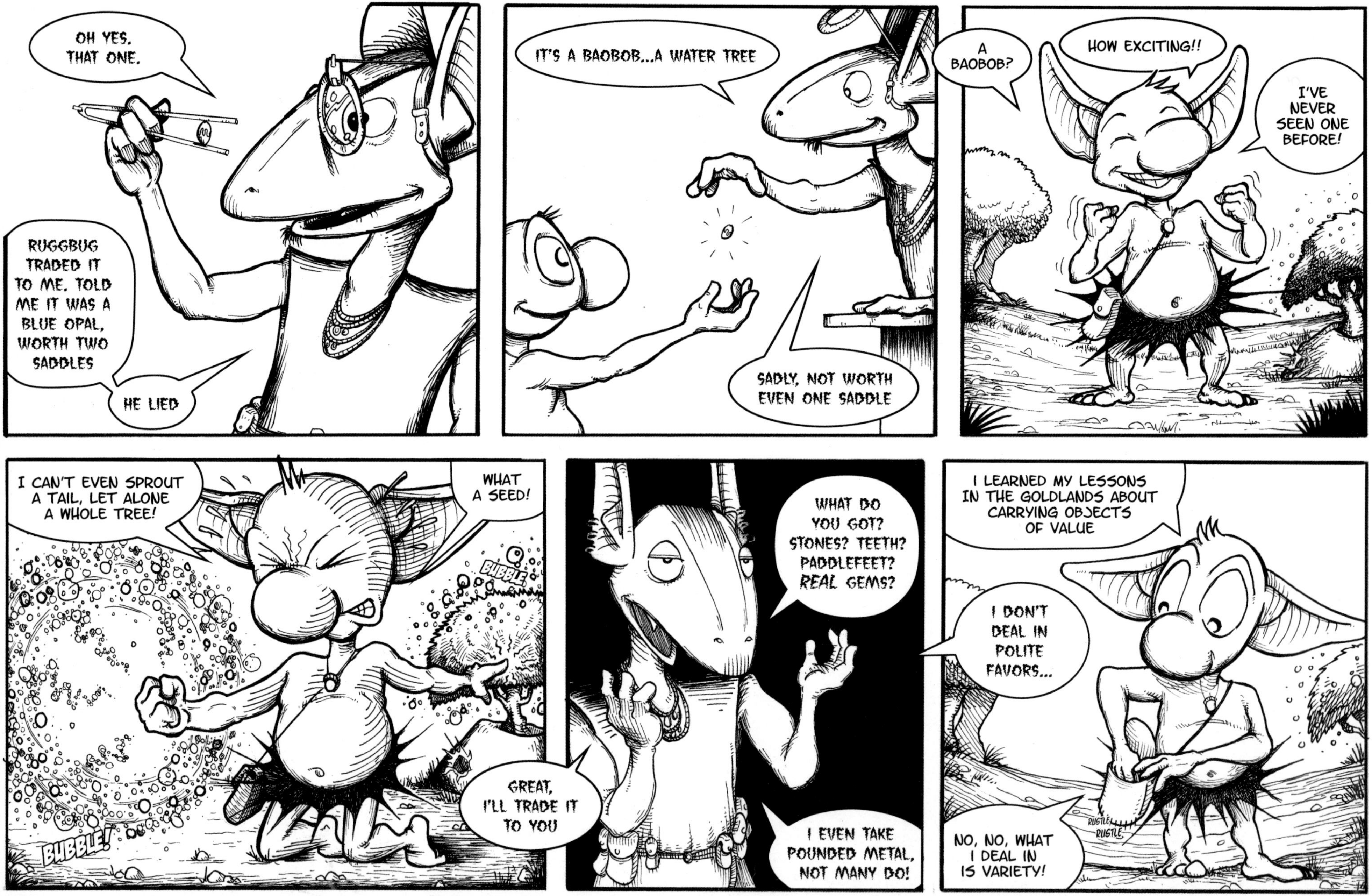
OH YES. THAT ONE.
RUGGBUG TRADED IT TO ME. TOLD ME IT WAS A BLUE OPAL, WORTH TWO SADDLES
HE LIED
IT'S A BAOBOB...A WATER TREE
SADLY, NOT WORTH EVEN ONE SADDLE
A BAOBOB?
HOW EXCITING!!
I'VE NEVER SEEN ONE BEFORE!
I CAN'T EVEN SPROUT A TAIL, LET ALONE A WHOLE TREE!
WHAT A SEED!
BUBBLE
BUBBLE!
GREAT, I'LL TRADE IT TO YOU
WHAT DO YOU GOT? STONES? TEETH? PADDLEFEET? *REAL* GEMS?
I EVEN TAKE POUNDED METAL, NOT MANY DO!
I LEARNED MY LESSONS IN THE GOLDLANDS ABOUT CARRYING OBJECTS OF VALUE
I DON'T DEAL IN POLITE FAVORS...
RUSTLE RUSTLE
NO, NO, WHAT I DEAL IN IS VARIETY!

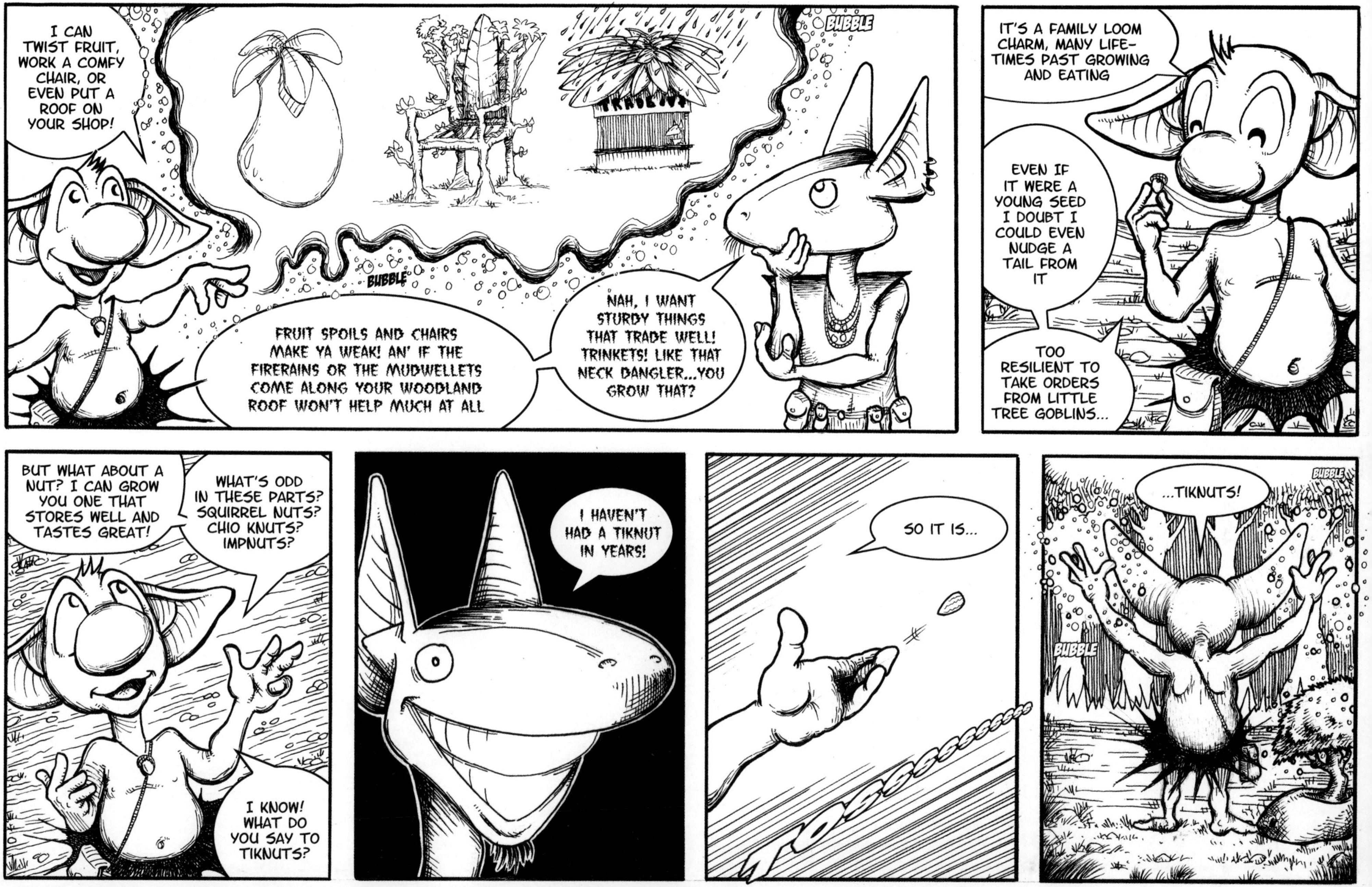
I CAN TWIST FRUIT, WORK A COMFY CHAIR, OR EVEN PUT A ROOF ON YOUR SHOP!
BUBBLE
BUBBLE
FRUIT SPOILS AND CHAIRS MAKE YA WEAK! AN' IF THE FIRERAINS OR THE MUDWELLETS COME ALONG YOUR WOODLAND ROOF WON'T HELP MUCH AT ALL
NAH, I WANT STURDY THINGS THAT TRADE WELL! TRINKETS! LIKE THAT NECK DANGLER...YOU GROW THAT?
IT'S A FAMILY LOOM CHARM, MANY LIFE-TIMES PAST GROWING AND EATING
EVEN IF IT WERE A YOUNG SEED I DOUBT I COULD EVEN NUDGE A TAIL FROM IT
TOO RESILIENT TO TAKE ORDERS FROM LITTLE TREE GOBLINS...
BUT WHAT ABOUT A NUT? I CAN GROW YOU ONE THAT STORES WELL AND TASTES GREAT!
WHAT'S ODD IN THESE PARTS? SQUIRREL NUTS? CHIO KNUTS? IMPNUTS?
I KNOW! WHAT DO YOU SAY TO TIKNUTS?
I HAVEN'T HAD A TIKNUT IN YEARS!
SO IT IS...
TOSSSSSSSSSS
BUBBLE
...TIKNUTS!
BUBBLE

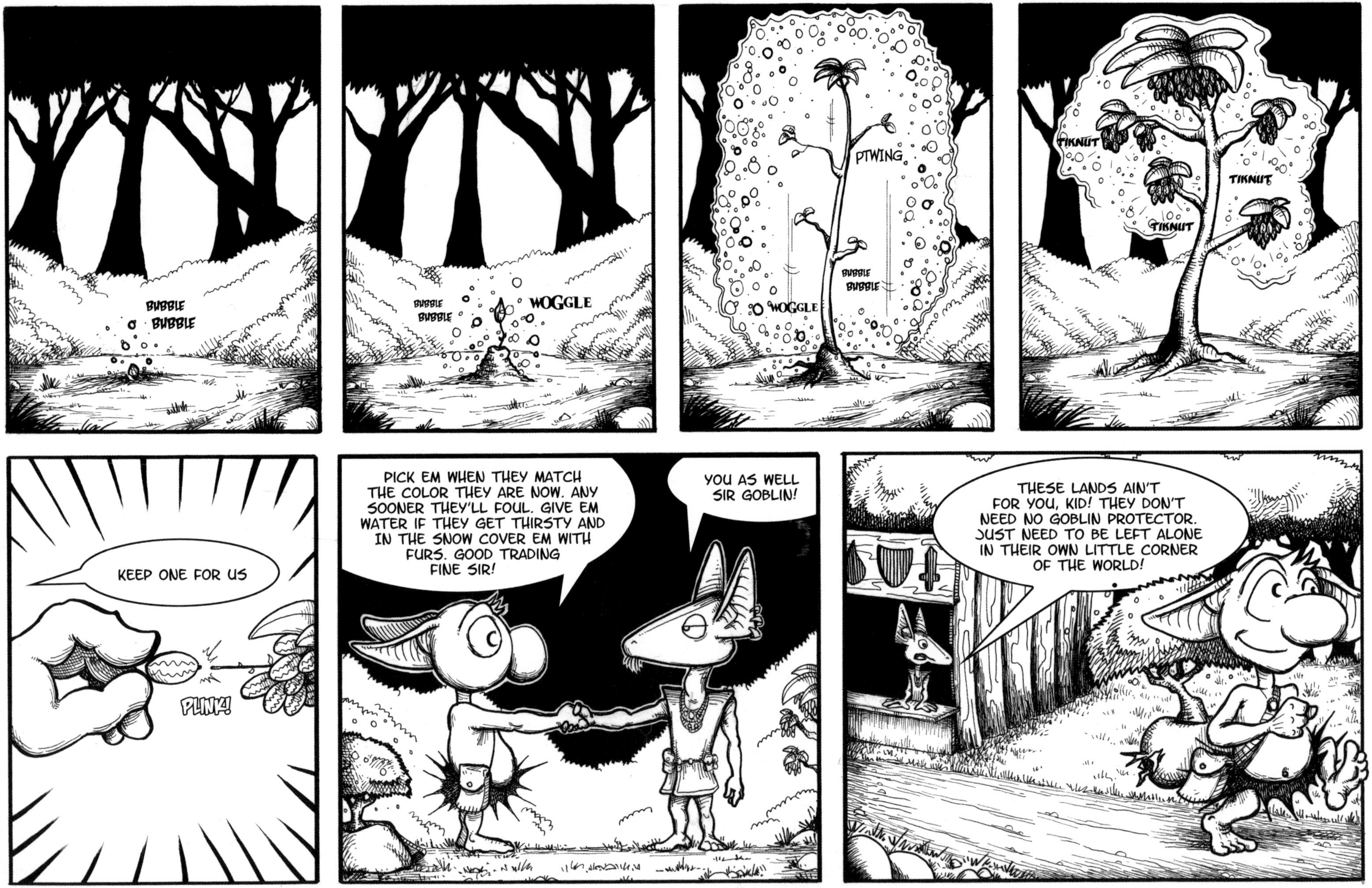
BUBBLE
BUBBLE
BUBBLE
BUBBLE
WOGGLE
WOGGLE
PTWING
BUBBLE
BUBBLE
TIKNUT
TIKNUT
TIKNUT
KEEP ONE FOR US
PLINK!
PICK EM WHEN THEY MATCH THE COLOR THEY ARE NOW. ANY SOONER THEY'LL FOUL. GIVE EM WATER IF THEY GET THIRSTY AND IN THE SNOW COVER EM WITH FURS. GOOD TRADING FINE SIR!
YOU AS WELL SIR GOBLIN!
THESE LANDS AIN'T FOR YOU, KID! THEY DON'T NEED NO GOBLIN PROTECTOR. JUST NEED TO BE LEFT ALONE IN THEIR OWN LITTLE CORNER OF THE WORLD!

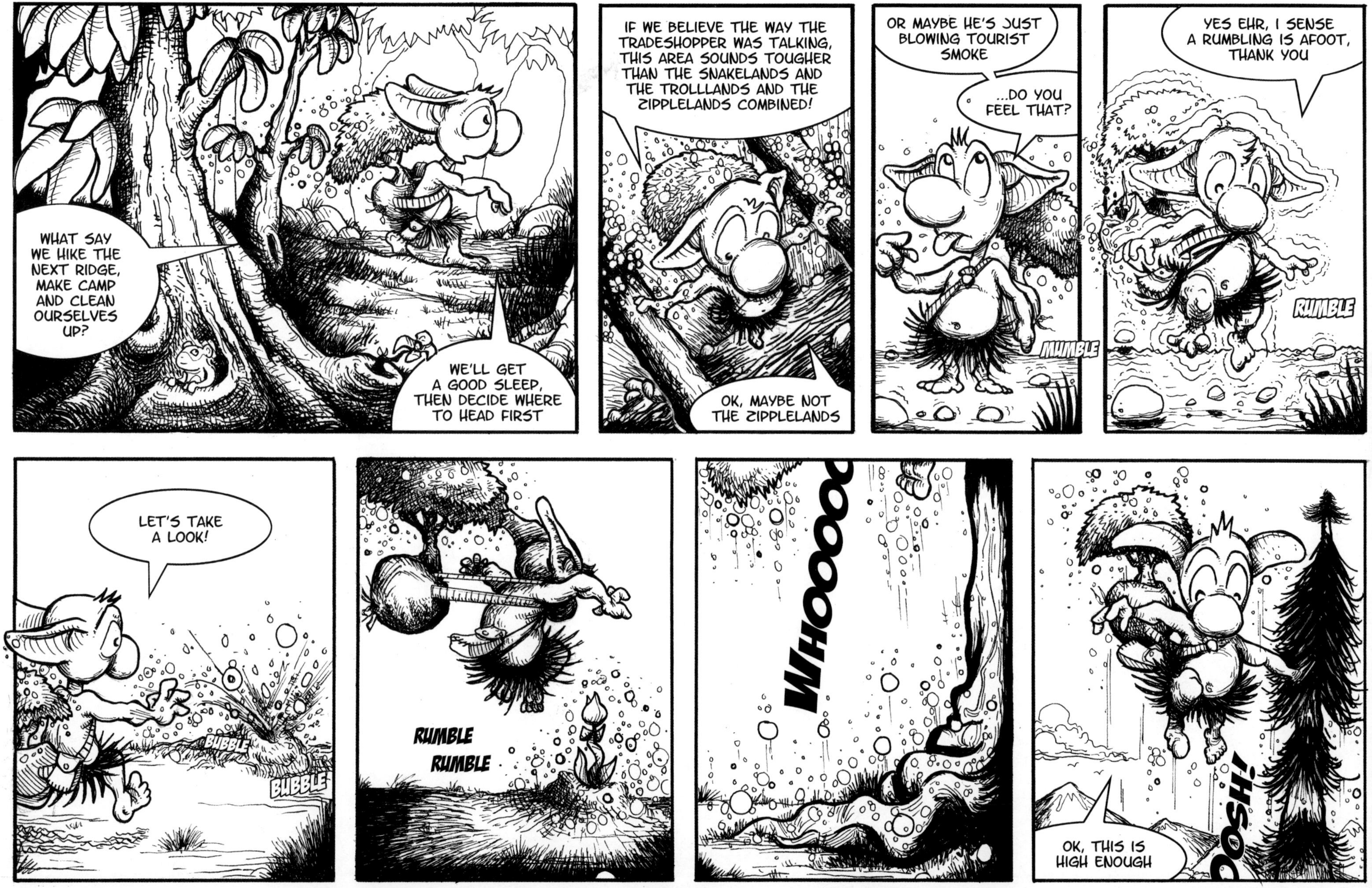
WHAT SAY WE HIKE THE NEXT RIDGE, MAKE CAMP AND CLEAN OURSELVES UP?
WE'LL GET A GOOD SLEEP, THEN DECIDE WHERE TO HEAD FIRST
IF WE BELIEVE THE WAY THE TRADESHOPPER WAS TALKING, THIS AREA SOUNDS TOUGHER THAN THE SNAKELANDS AND THE TROLLLANDS AND THE ZIPPLELANDS COMBINED!
OK, MAYBE NOT THE ZIPPLELANDS
OR MAYBE HE'S JUST BLOWING TOURIST SMOKE
...DO YOU FEEL THAT?
MUMBLE
YES EHR, I SENSE A RUMBLING IS AFOOT, THANK YOU
RUMBLE
LET'S TAKE A LOOK!
BUBBLE
BUBBLE
RUMBLE
RUMBLE
WHOOOOO
OK, THIS IS HIGH ENOUGH
OOSH!

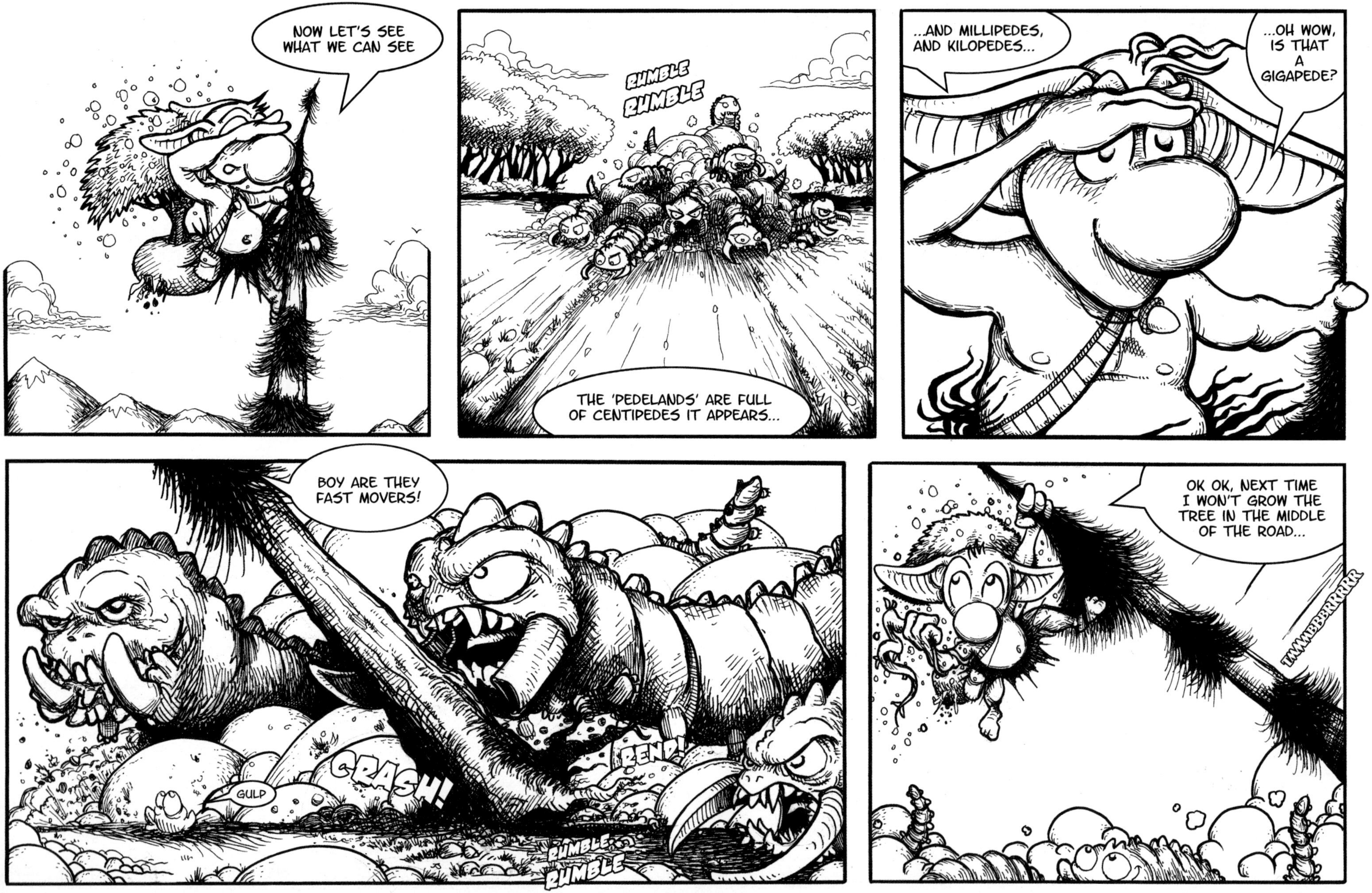
NOW LET'S SEE WHAT WE CAN SEE
RUMBLE
RUMBLE
THE 'PEDELANDS' ARE FULL OF CENTIPEDES IT APPEARS...
...AND MILLIPEDES, AND KILOPEDES...
...OH WOW, IS THAT A GIGAPEDE?
BOY ARE THEY FAST MOVERS!
CRASH!
BEND!
GULP
RUMBLE
RUMBLE
OK OK, NEXT TIME I WON'T GROW THE TREE IN THE MIDDLE OF THE ROAD...
TWWWBBBRRRRR

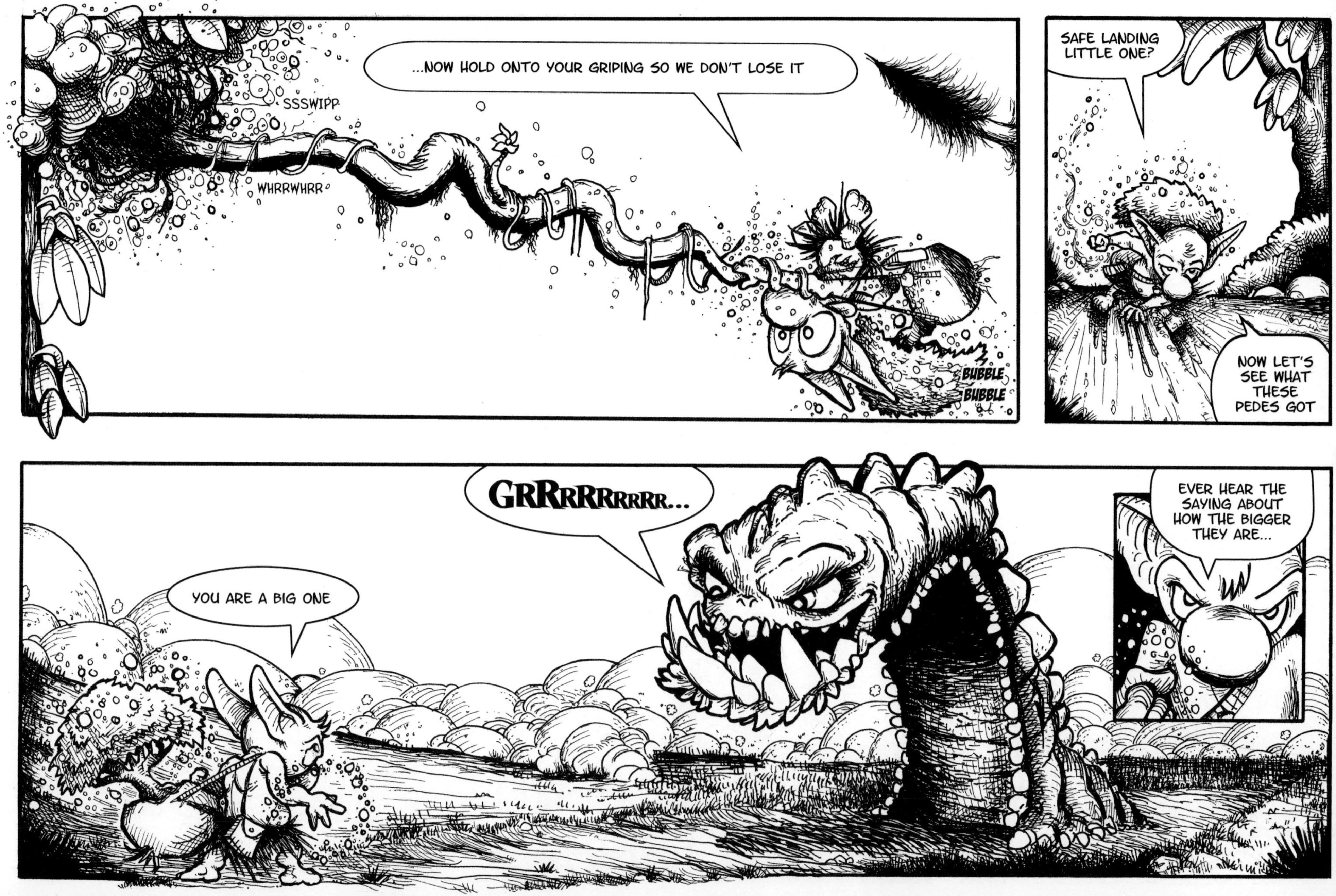
SSSWIPP
WHRRWHRR
...NOW HOLD ONTO YOUR GRIPING SO WE DON'T LOSE IT
BUBBLE
BUBBLE
SAFE LANDING LITTLE ONE?
NOW LET'S SEE WHAT THESE PEDES GOT
YOU ARE A BIG ONE
GRRRRRRRRRR...
EVER HEAR THE SAYING ABOUT HOW THE BIGGER THEY ARE...

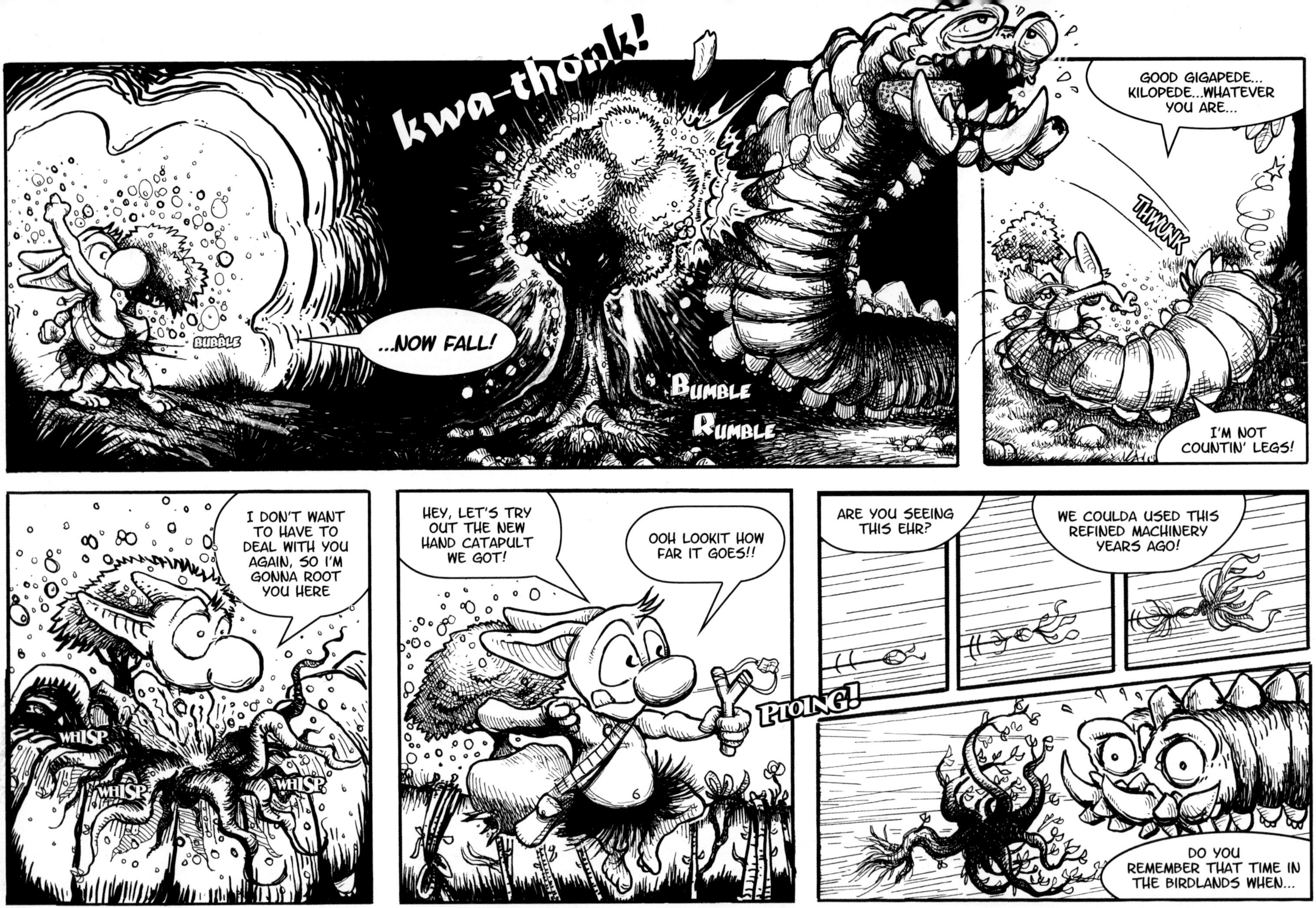
kwa-thonk!
BUBBLE
...NOW FALL!
BUMBLE
RUMBLE
GOOD GIGAPEDE... KILOPEDE...WHATEVER YOU ARE...
THWUNK
I'M NOT COUNTIN' LEGS!
I DON'T WANT TO HAVE TO DEAL WITH YOU AGAIN, SO I'M GONNA ROOT YOU HERE
WHISP
WHISP
WHISP
HEY, LET'S TRY OUT THE NEW HAND CATAPULT WE GOT!
OOH LOOKIT HOW FAR IT GOES!!
PTOING!
ARE YOU SEEING THIS EHR?
WE COULDA USED THIS REFINED MACHINERY YEARS AGO!
DO YOU REMEMBER THAT TIME IN THE BIRDLANDS WHEN...

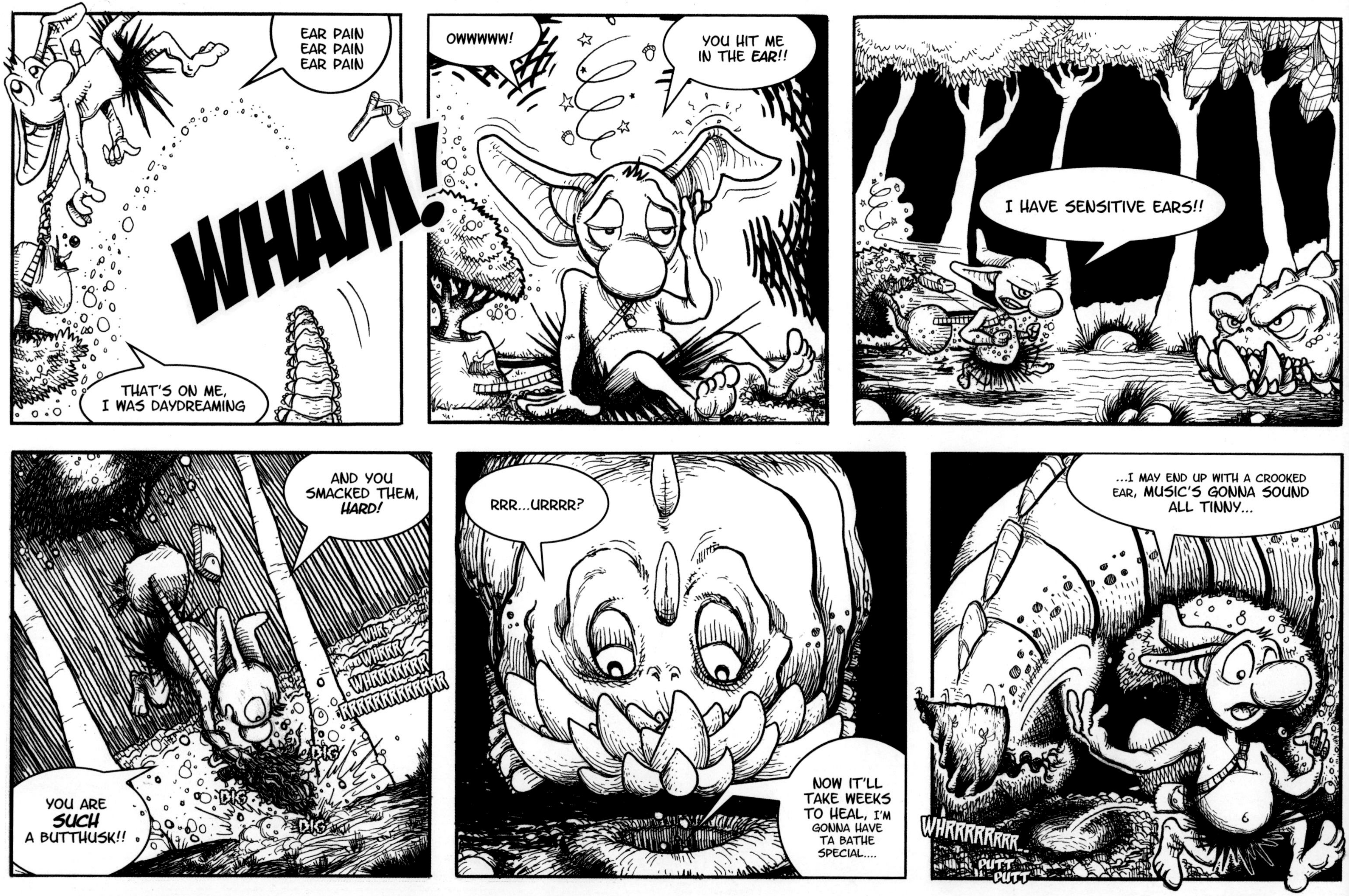
EAR PAIN
EAR PAIN
EAR PAIN
WHAM!
THAT'S ON ME,
I WAS DAYDREAMING
OWWWWW!
YOU HIT ME
IN THE EAR!!
I HAVE SENSITIVE EARS!!
AND YOU
SMACKED THEM,
HARD!
WHR
WHRRR
WHRRRRRRR
WHRRRRRRRRR
RRRRRRRRRRRR
DIG
DIG
DIG
YOU ARE
SUCH
A BUTTHUSK!!
RRR...URRRR?
NOW IT'LL
TAKE WEEKS
TO HEAL, I'M
GONNA HAVE
TA BATHE
SPECIAL....
...I MAY END UP WITH A CROOKED
EAR, MUSIC'S GONNA SOUND
ALL TINNY...
WHRRRRRRRR
PUTT
PUTT

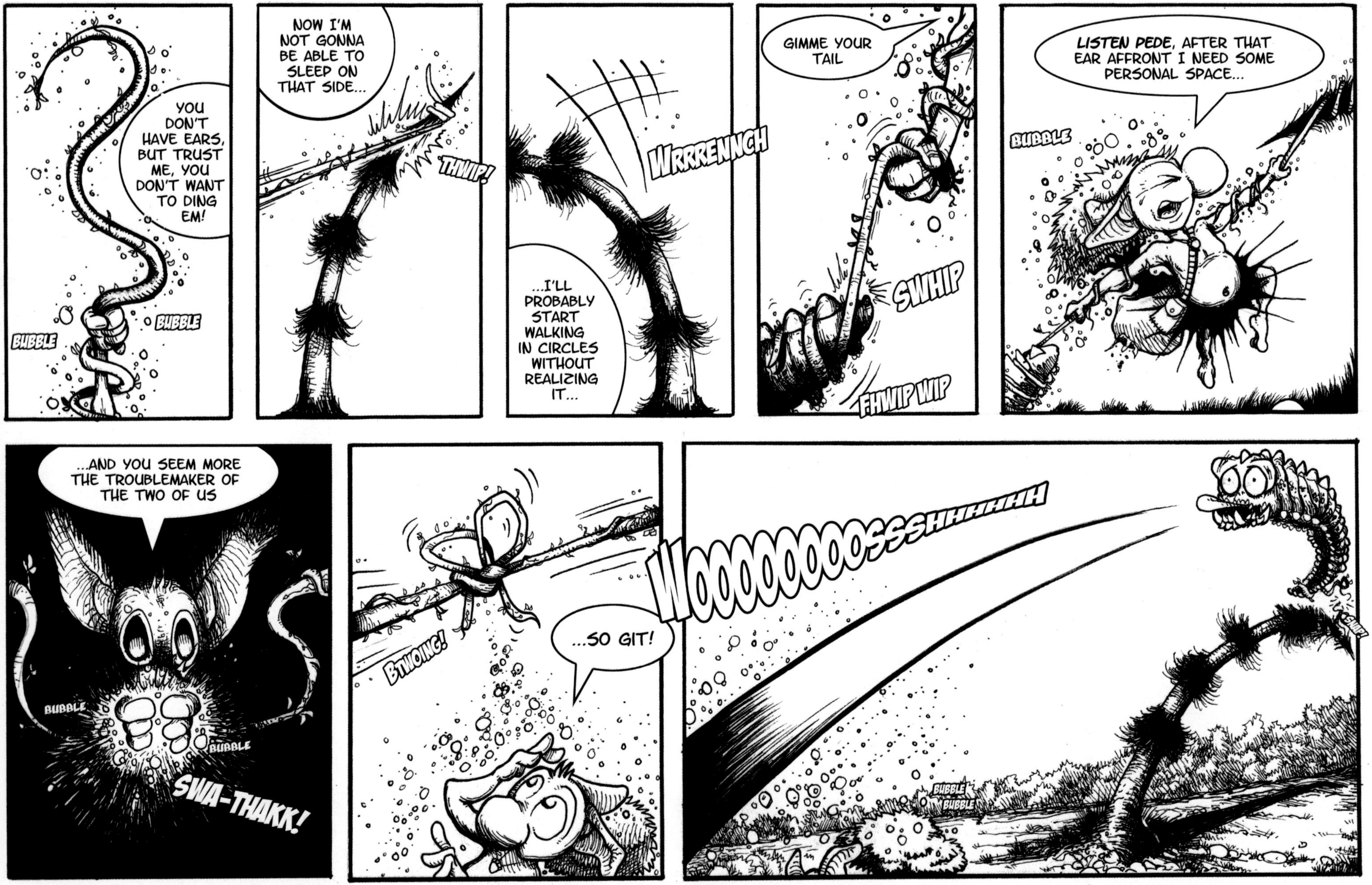
YOU DON'T HAVE EARS, BUT TRUST ME, YOU DON'T WANT TO DING EM!
BUBBLE
BUBBLE
NOW I'M NOT GONNA BE ABLE TO SLEEP ON THAT SIDE...
THWIP!
WRRRENNCH
...I'LL PROBABLY START WALKING IN CIRCLES WITHOUT REALIZING IT...
GIMME YOUR TAIL
SWHIP
FHWIP WIP
LISTEN PEDE, AFTER THAT EAR AFFRONT I NEED SOME PERSONAL SPACE...
BUBBLE
...AND YOU SEEM MORE THE TROUBLEMAKER OF THE TWO OF US
BUBBLE
BUBBLE
SWA-THAKK!
BTWOING!
...SO GIT!
WOOOOOOOOSSSHHHHHH
BUBBLE
BUBBLE

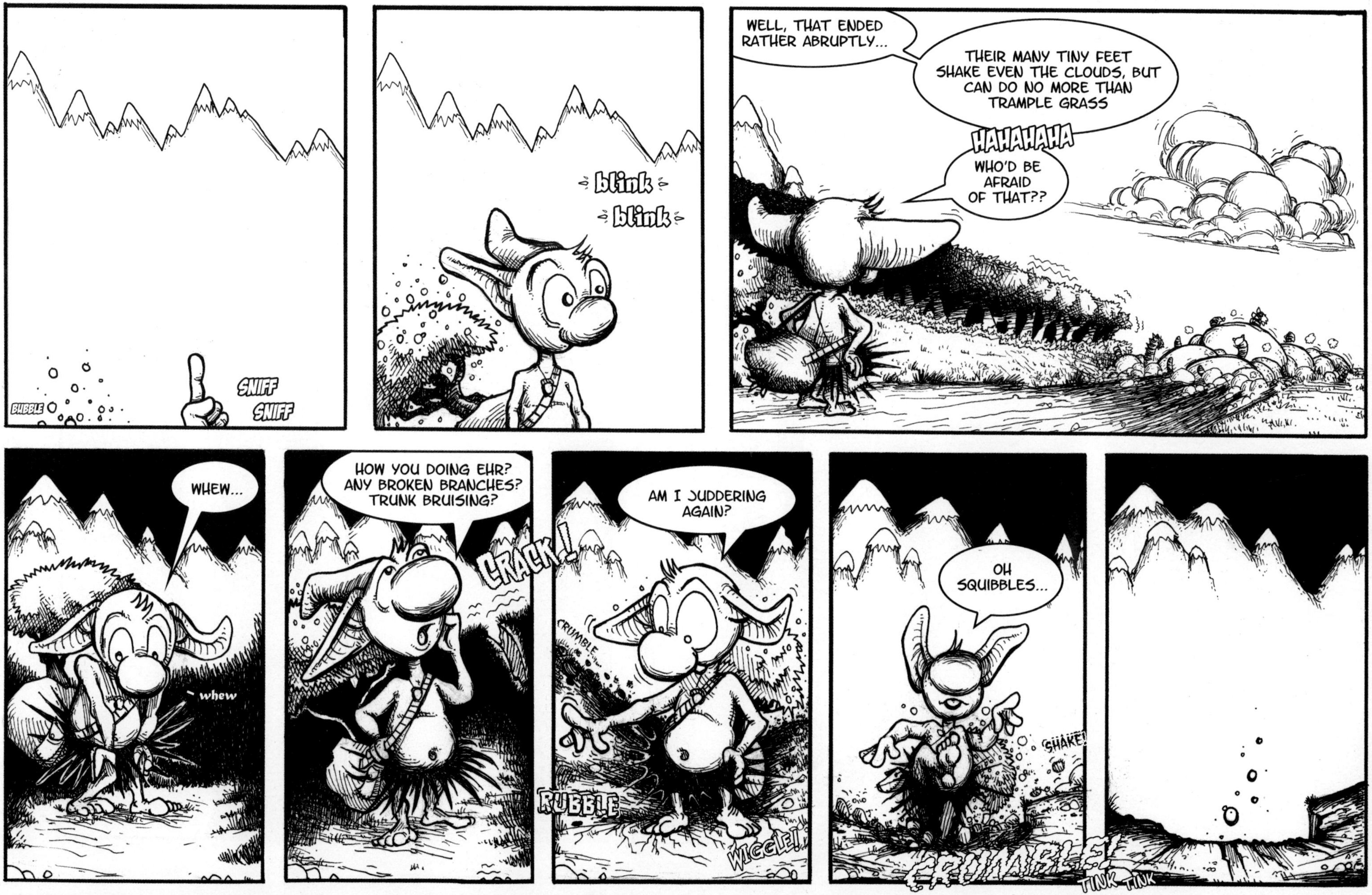
BUBBLE
SNIFF
SNIFF
blink
blink
WELL, THAT ENDED RATHER ABRUPTLY...
THEIR MANY TINY FEET SHAKE EVEN THE CLOUDS, BUT CAN DO NO MORE THAN TRAMPLE GRASS
HAHAHAHA
WHO'D BE AFRAID OF THAT??
WHEW...
whew
HOW YOU DOING EHR? ANY BROKEN BRANCHES? TRUNK BRUISING?
CRACK!
AM I JUDDERING AGAIN?
CRUMBLE
RUBBLE
WIGGLE!
OH SQUIBBLES...
SHAKE!
CRUMBLE!
TINK TINK

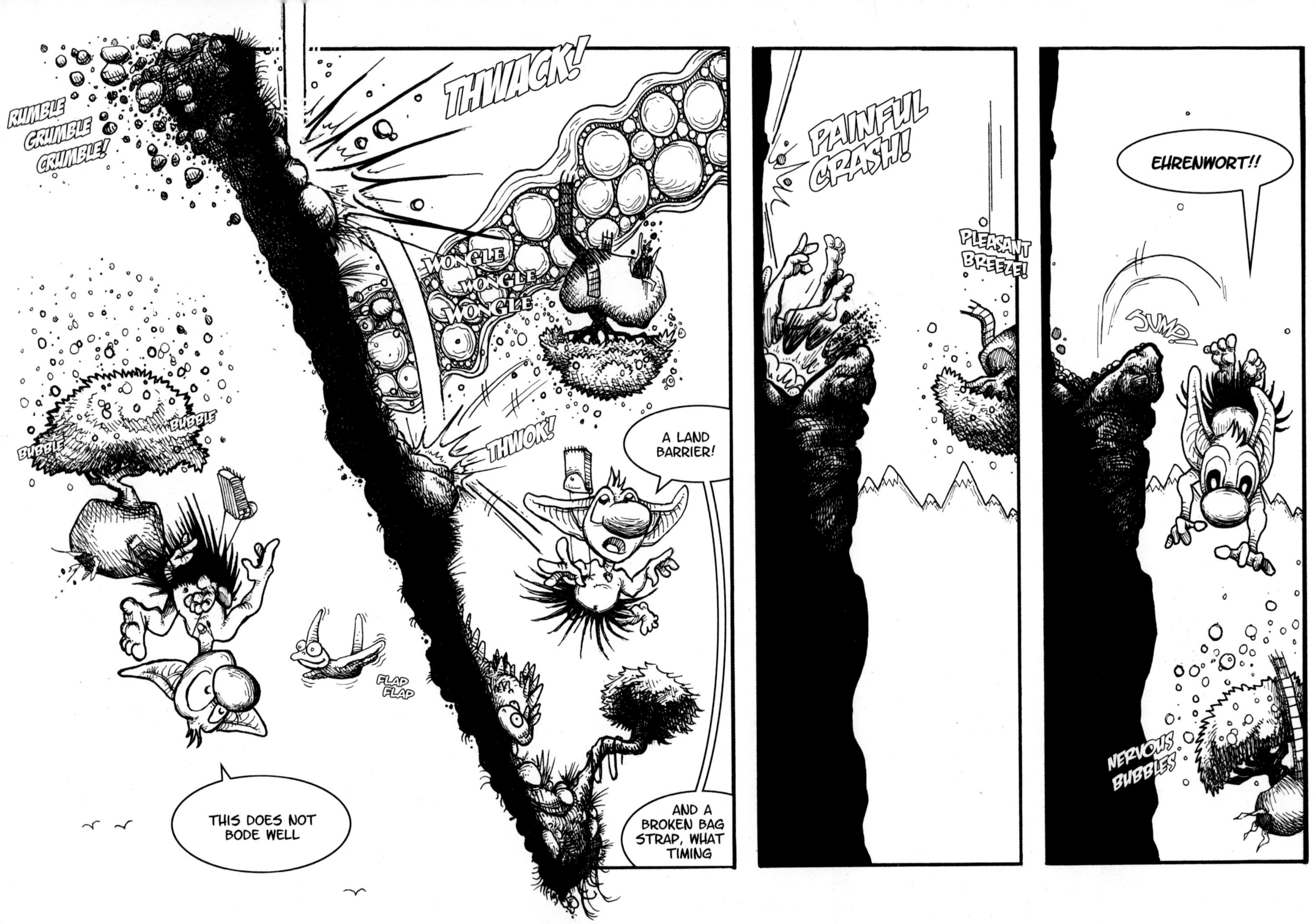
RUMBLE
CRUMBLE
CRUMBLE!
THWACK!
WONGLE
WONGLE
WONGLE
BUBBLE
BUBBLE
THWOK!
A LAND BARRIER!
FLAP
FLAP
THIS DOES NOT BODE WELL
AND A BROKEN BAG STRAP, WHAT TIMING
PAINFUL CRASH!
PLEASANT BREEZE!
EHRENWORT!!
JUMP!
NERVOUS BUBBLES

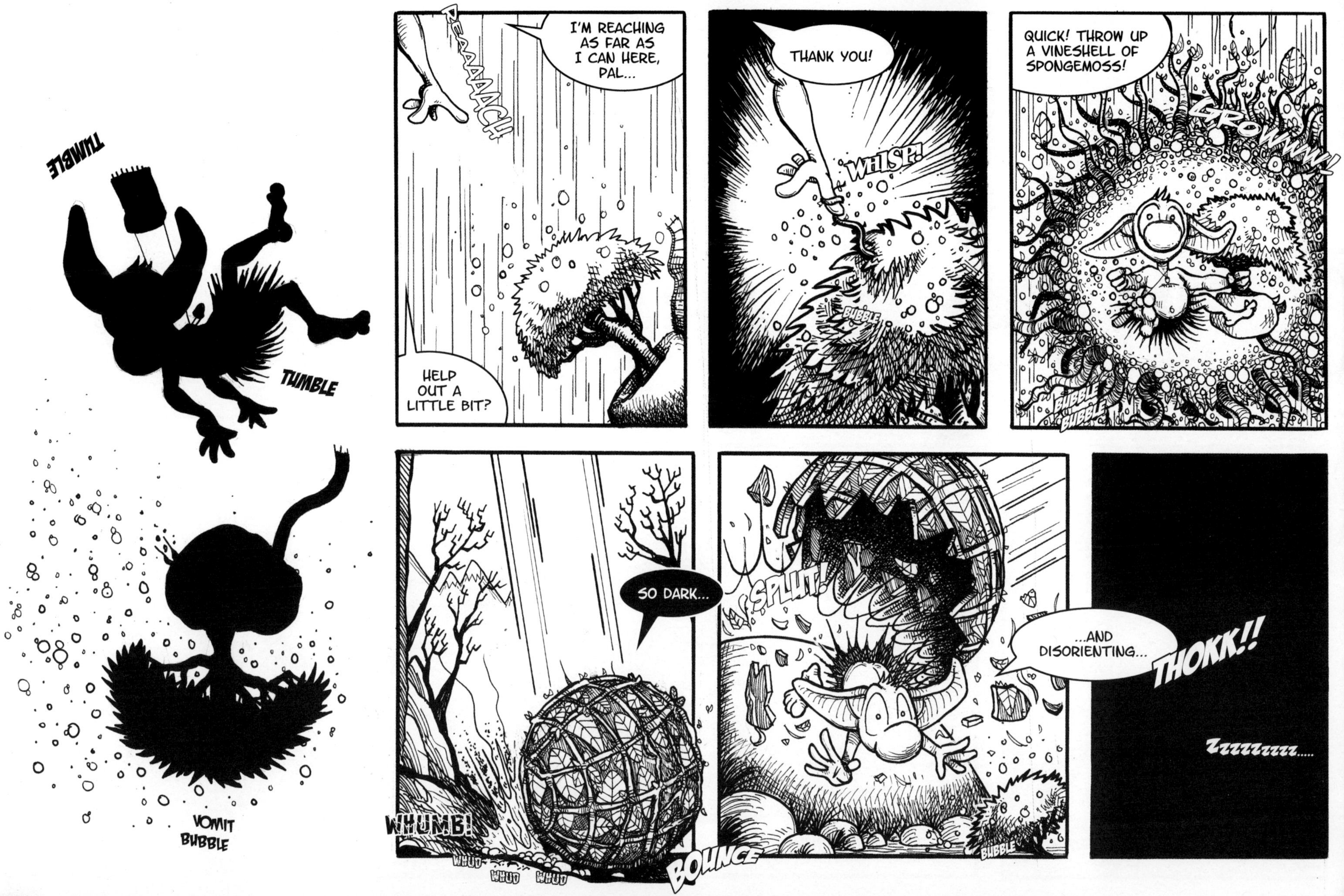
TUMBLE
TUMBLE
VOMIT
BUBBLE
REAAAAACH!
I'M REACHING AS FAR AS I CAN HERE, PAL...
HELP OUT A LITTLE BIT?
THANK YOU!
WHISP!
BUBBLE
QUICK! THROW UP A VINESHELL OF SPONGEMOSS!
GROWWW!
BUBBLE
BUBBLE
SO DARK...
WHUMB!
WHUD
WHUD
WHUD
BOUNCE
SPLUT!
...AND DISORIENTING...
BUBBLE
THOKK!!
Zzzzzzzzz.....

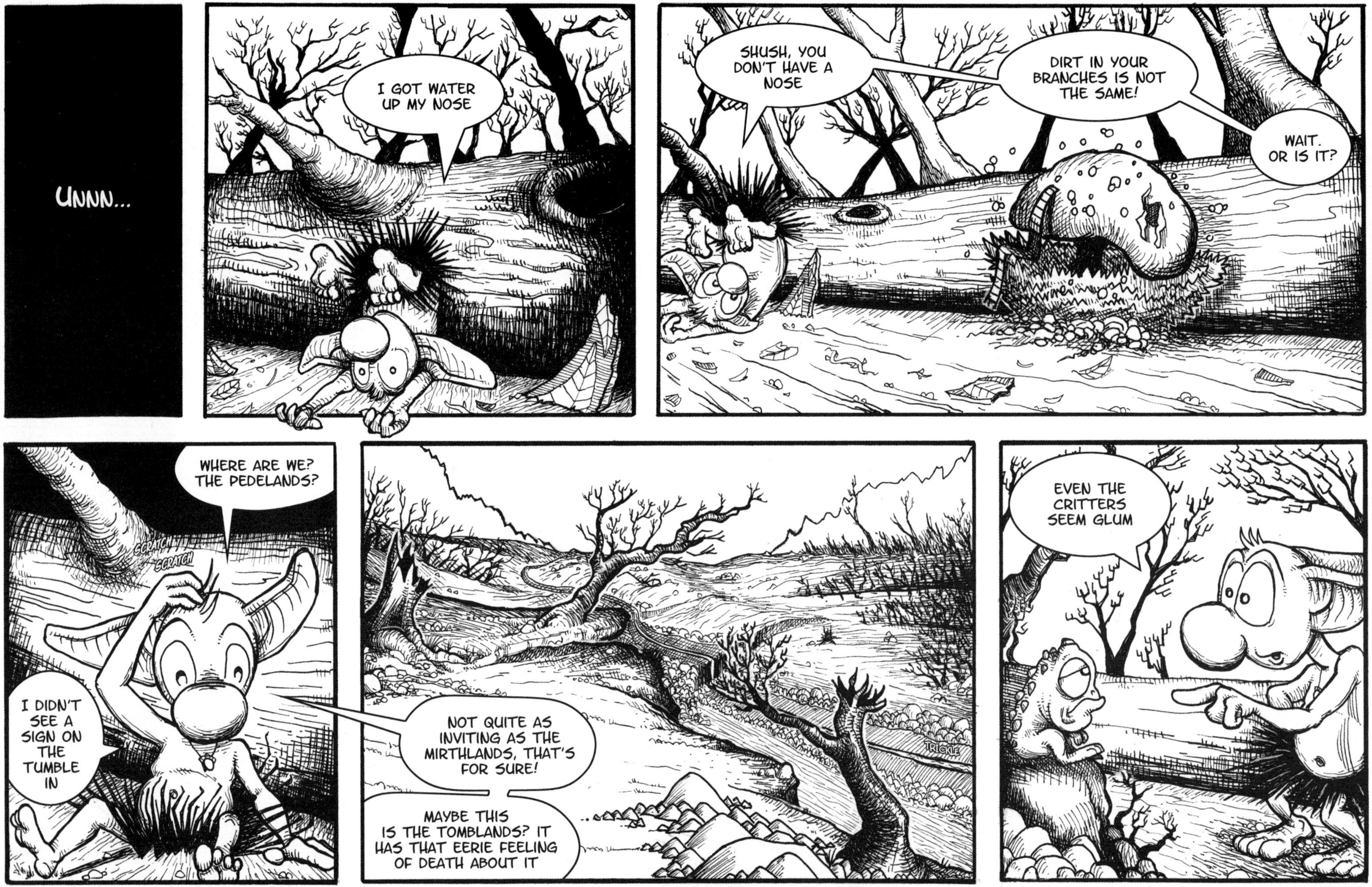
UNNN...
I GOT WATER UP MY NOSE
SHUSH, YOU DON'T HAVE A NOSE
DIRT IN YOUR BRANCHES IS NOT THE SAME!
WAIT. OR IS IT?
WHERE ARE WE? THE PEDELANDS?
SCRATCH
SCRATCH
I DIDN'T SEE A SIGN ON THE TUMBLE IN
NOT QUITE AS INVITING AS THE MIRTHLANDS, THAT'S FOR SURE!
MAYBE THIS IS THE TOMBLANDS? IT HAS THAT EERIE FEELING OF DEATH ABOUT IT
TRICKLE
EVEN THE CRITTERS SEEM GLUM

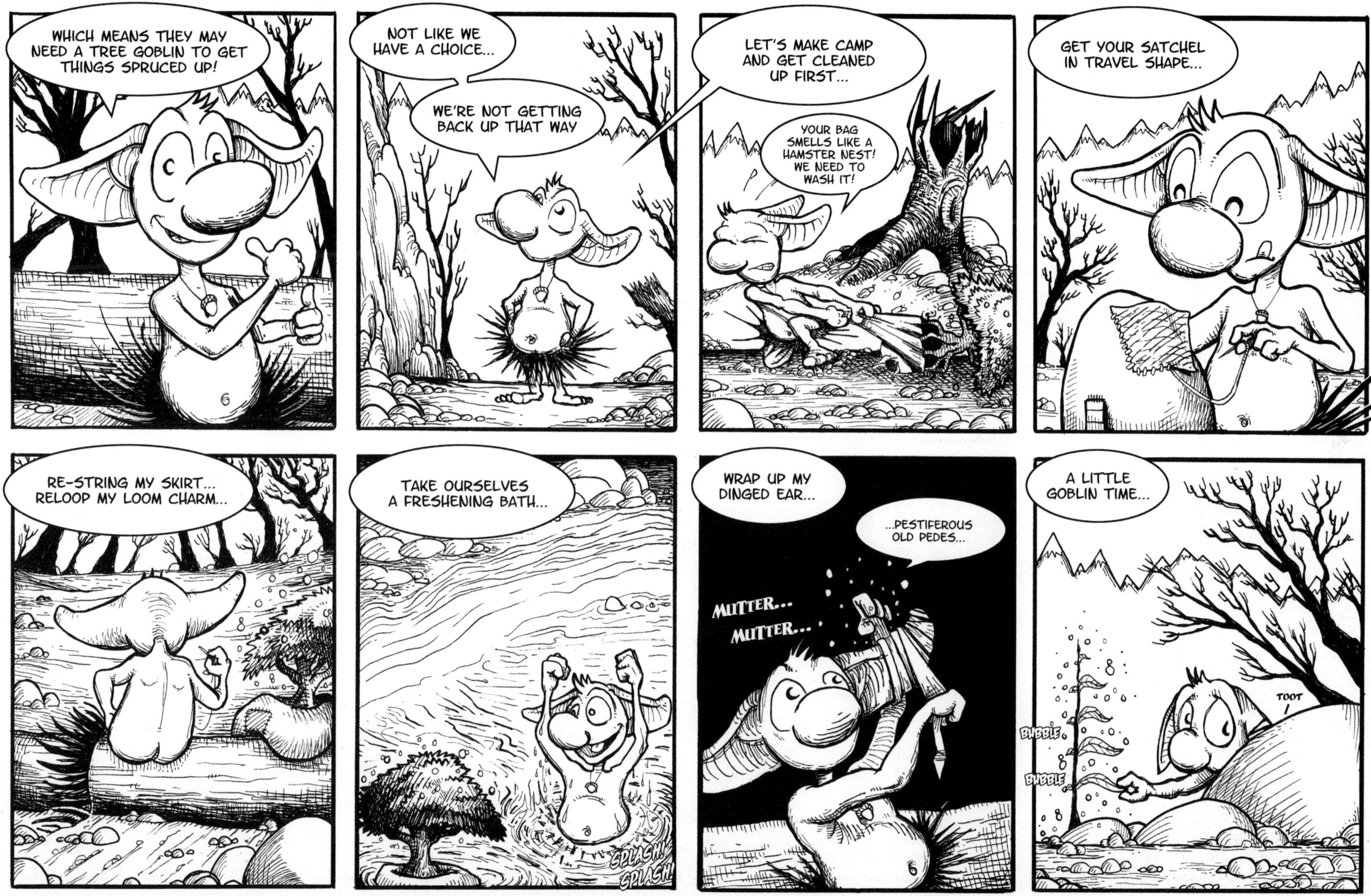

WHICH MEANS THEY MAY NEED A TREE GOBLIN TO GET THINGS SPRUCED UP!
NOT LIKE WE HAVE A CHOICE...
WE'RE NOT GETTING BACK UP THAT WAY
LET'S MAKE CAMP AND GET CLEANED UP FIRST...
YOUR BAG SMELLS LIKE A HAMSTER NEST! WE NEED TO WASH IT!
GET YOUR SATCHEL IN TRAVEL SHAPE...
RE-STRING MY SKIRT... RELOOP MY LOOM CHARM...
TAKE OURSELVES A FRESHENING BATH...
SPLASH! SPLASH!
WRAP UP MY DINGED EAR...
...PESTIFEROUS OLD PEDES...
MUTTER... MUTTER...
A LITTLE GOBLIN TIME...
BUBBLE
BUBBLE
TOOT

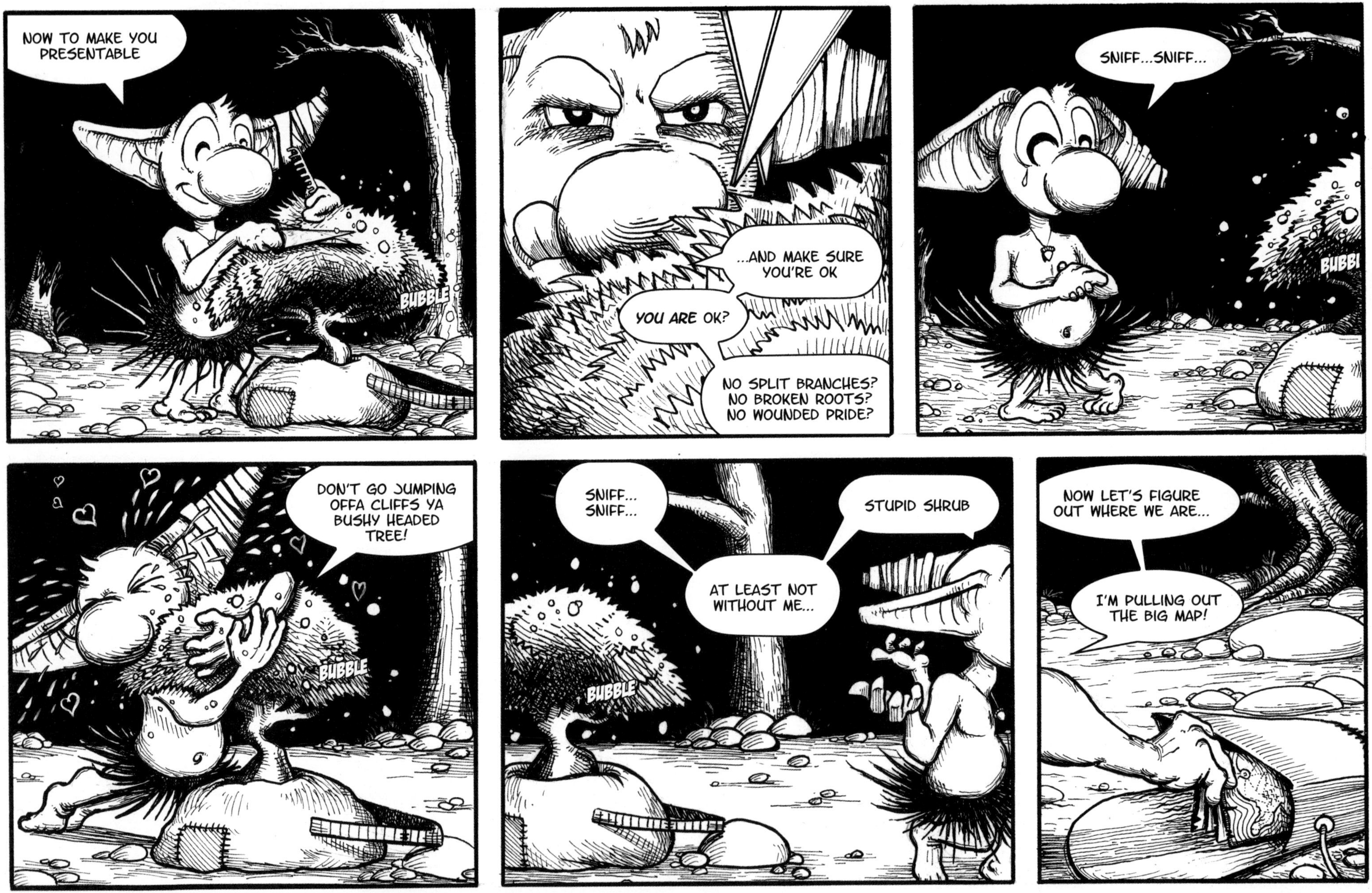
NOW TO MAKE YOU PRESENTABLE
BUBBLE
...AND MAKE SURE YOU'RE OK
YOU ARE OK?
NO SPLIT BRANCHES? NO BROKEN ROOTS? NO WOUNDED PRIDE?
SNIFF...SNIFF...
BUBBI
DON'T GO JUMPING OFFA CLIFFS YA BUSHY HEADED TREE!
BUBBLE
SNIFF... SNIFF...
AT LEAST NOT WITHOUT ME...
STUPID SHRUB
BUBBLE
NOW LET'S FIGURE OUT WHERE WE ARE...
I'M PULLING OUT THE BIG MAP!

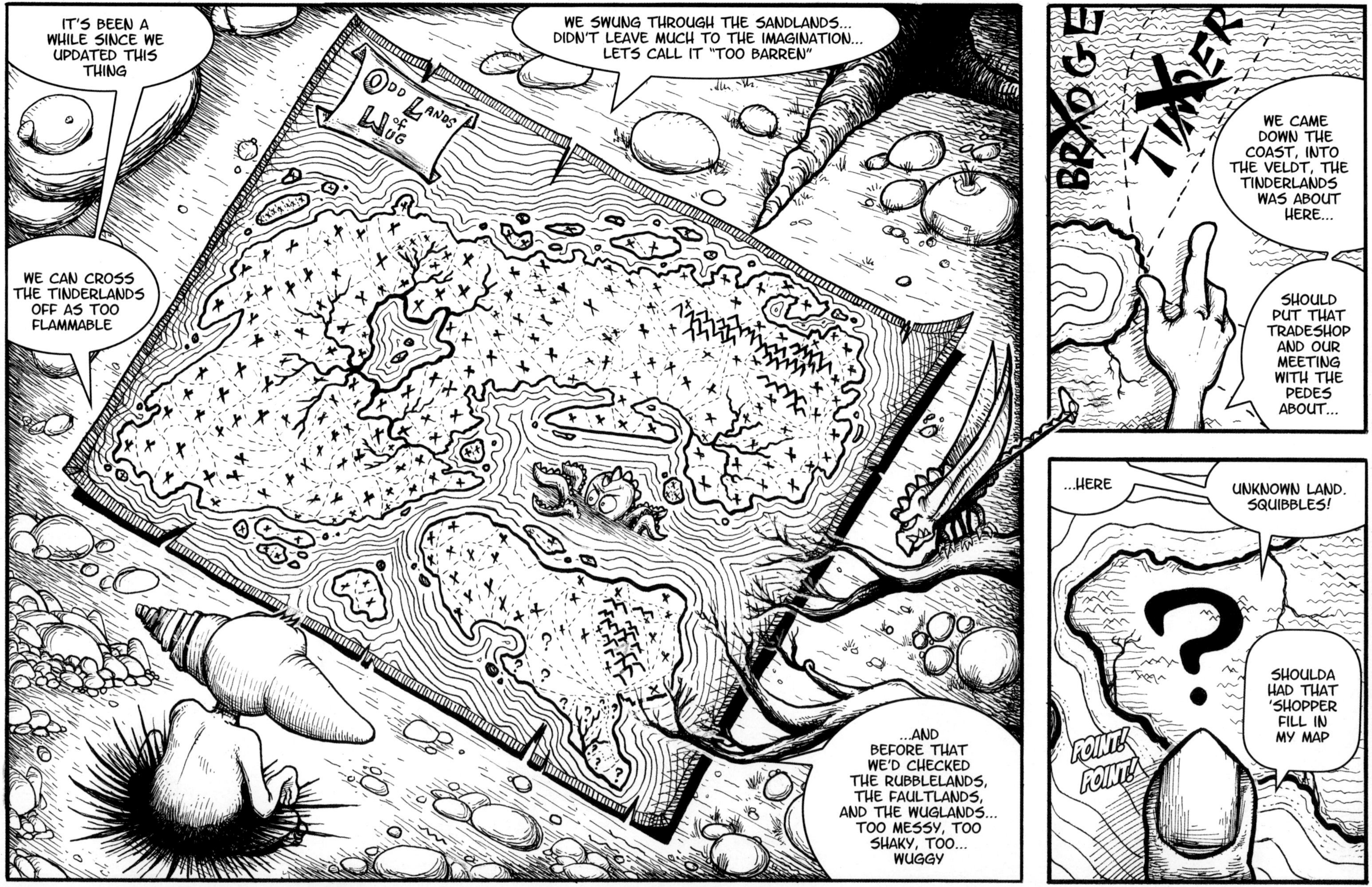
IT'S BEEN A WHILE SINCE WE UPDATED THIS THING
ODD LANDS of WUG
WE SWUNG THROUGH THE SANDLANDS... DIDN'T LEAVE MUCH TO THE IMAGINATION... LETS CALL IT "TOO BARREN"
WE CAN CROSS THE TINDERLANDS OFF AS TOO FLAMMABLE
...AND BEFORE THAT WE'D CHECKED THE RUBBLELANDS, THE FAULTLANDS, AND THE WUGLANDS... TOO MESSY, TOO SHAKY, TOO... WUGGY
BRIDGE
TIMBER
WE CAME DOWN THE COAST, INTO THE VELDT, THE TINDERLANDS WAS ABOUT HERE...
SHOULD PUT THAT TRADESHOP AND OUR MEETING WITH THE PEDES ABOUT...
...HERE
UNKNOWN LAND. SQUIBBLES!
?
POINT! POINT!
SHOULDA HAD THAT 'SHOPPER FILL IN MY MAP

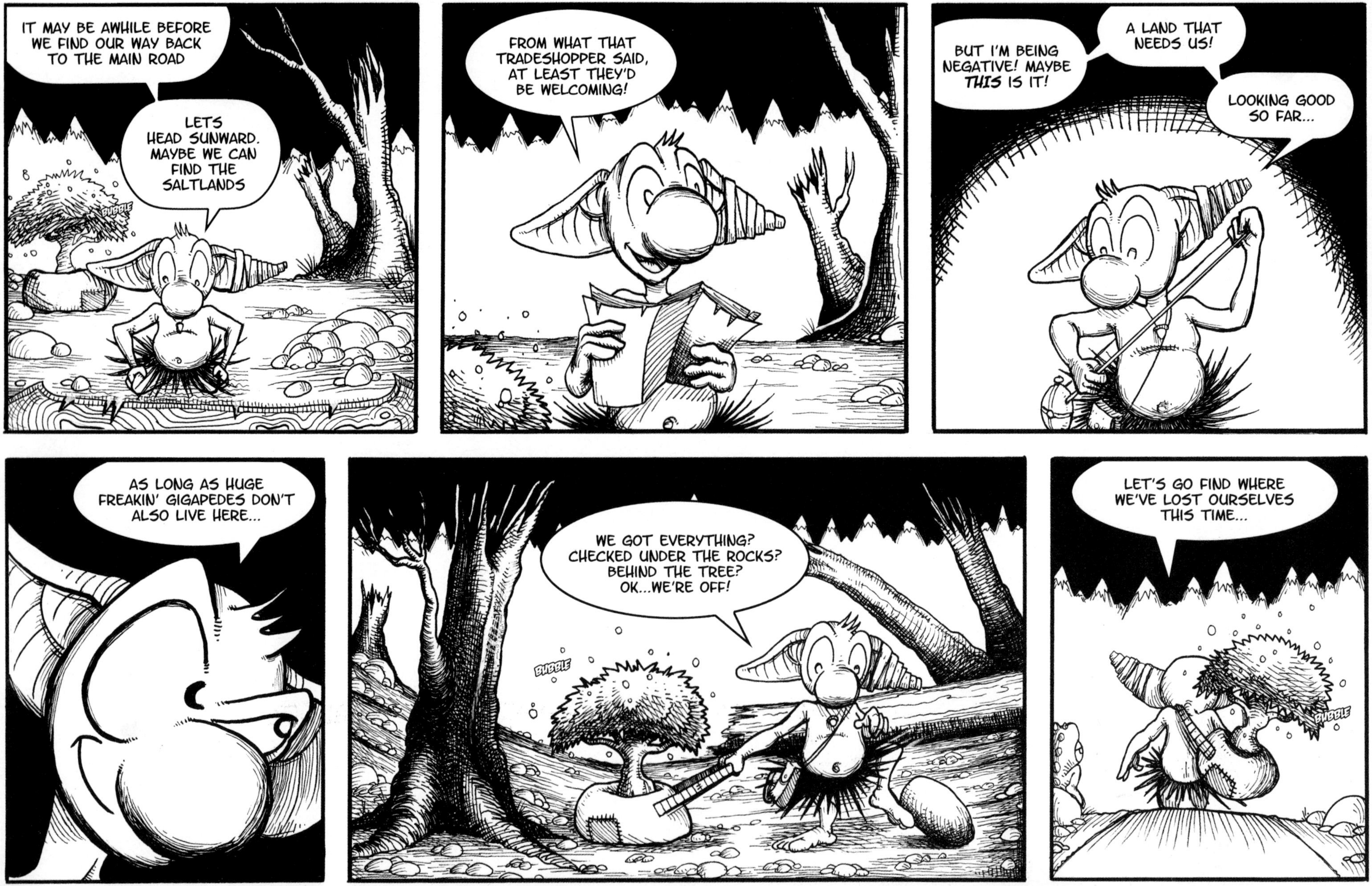
IT MAY BE AWHILE BEFORE WE FIND OUR WAY BACK TO THE MAIN ROAD
LETS HEAD SUNWARD. MAYBE WE CAN FIND THE SALTLANDS
BUBBLE
FROM WHAT THAT TRADESHOPPER SAID, AT LEAST THEY'D BE WELCOMING!
BUT I'M BEING NEGATIVE! MAYBE *THIS* IS IT!
A LAND THAT NEEDS US!
LOOKING GOOD SO FAR...
AS LONG AS HUGE FREAKIN' GIGAPEDES DON'T ALSO LIVE HERE...
WE GOT EVERYTHING? CHECKED UNDER THE ROCKS? BEHIND THE TREE? OK...WE'RE OFF!
BUBBLE
LET'S GO FIND WHERE WE'VE LOST OURSELVES THIS TIME...
BUBBLE

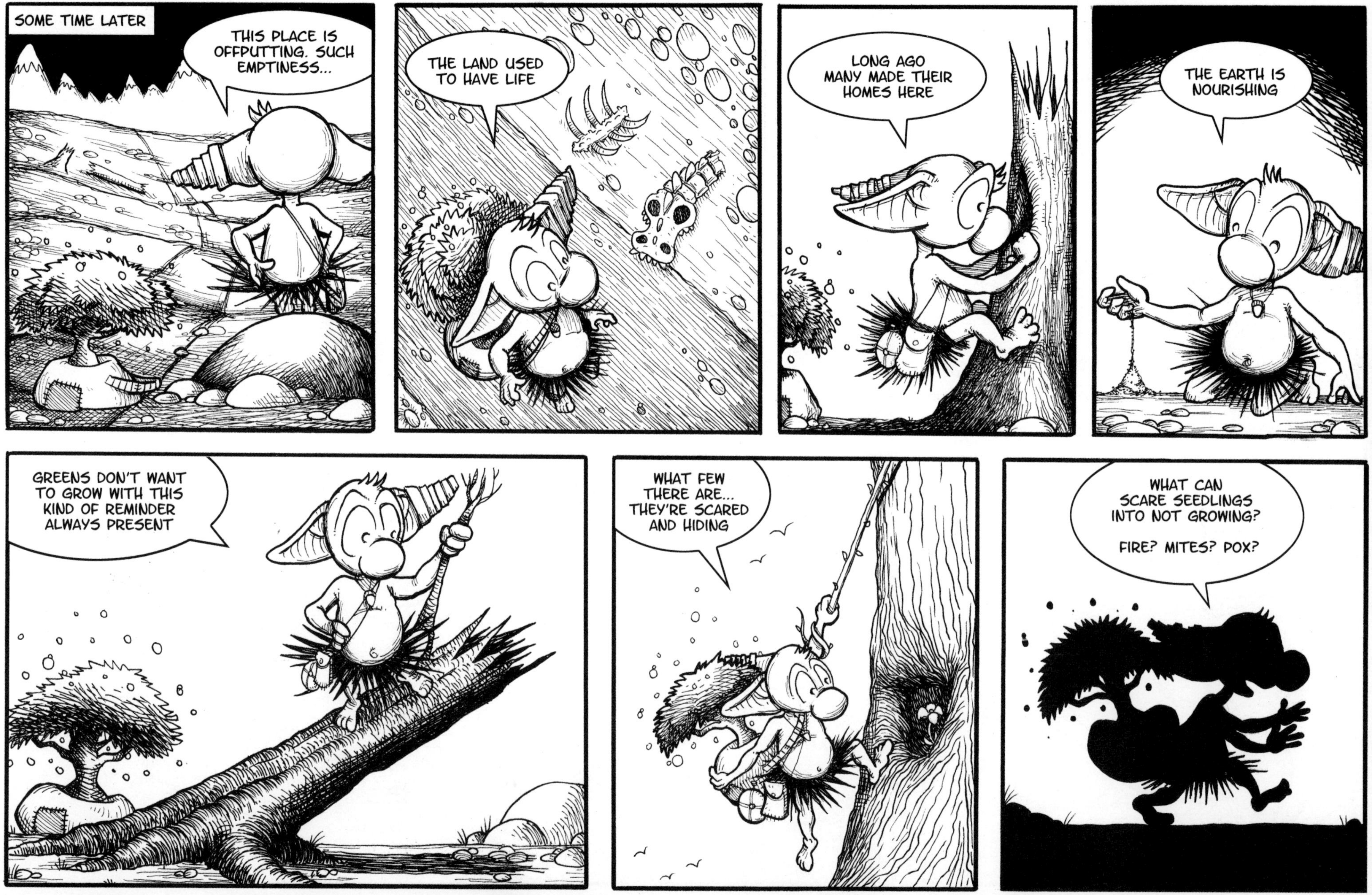
SOME TIME LATER
THIS PLACE IS OFFPUTTING. SUCH EMPTINESS...
THE LAND USED TO HAVE LIFE
LONG AGO MANY MADE THEIR HOMES HERE
THE EARTH IS NOURISHING
GREENS DON'T WANT TO GROW WITH THIS KIND OF REMINDER ALWAYS PRESENT
WHAT FEW THERE ARE... THEY'RE SCARED AND HIDING
WHAT CAN SCARE SEEDLINGS INTO NOT GROWING?
FIRE? MITES? POX?

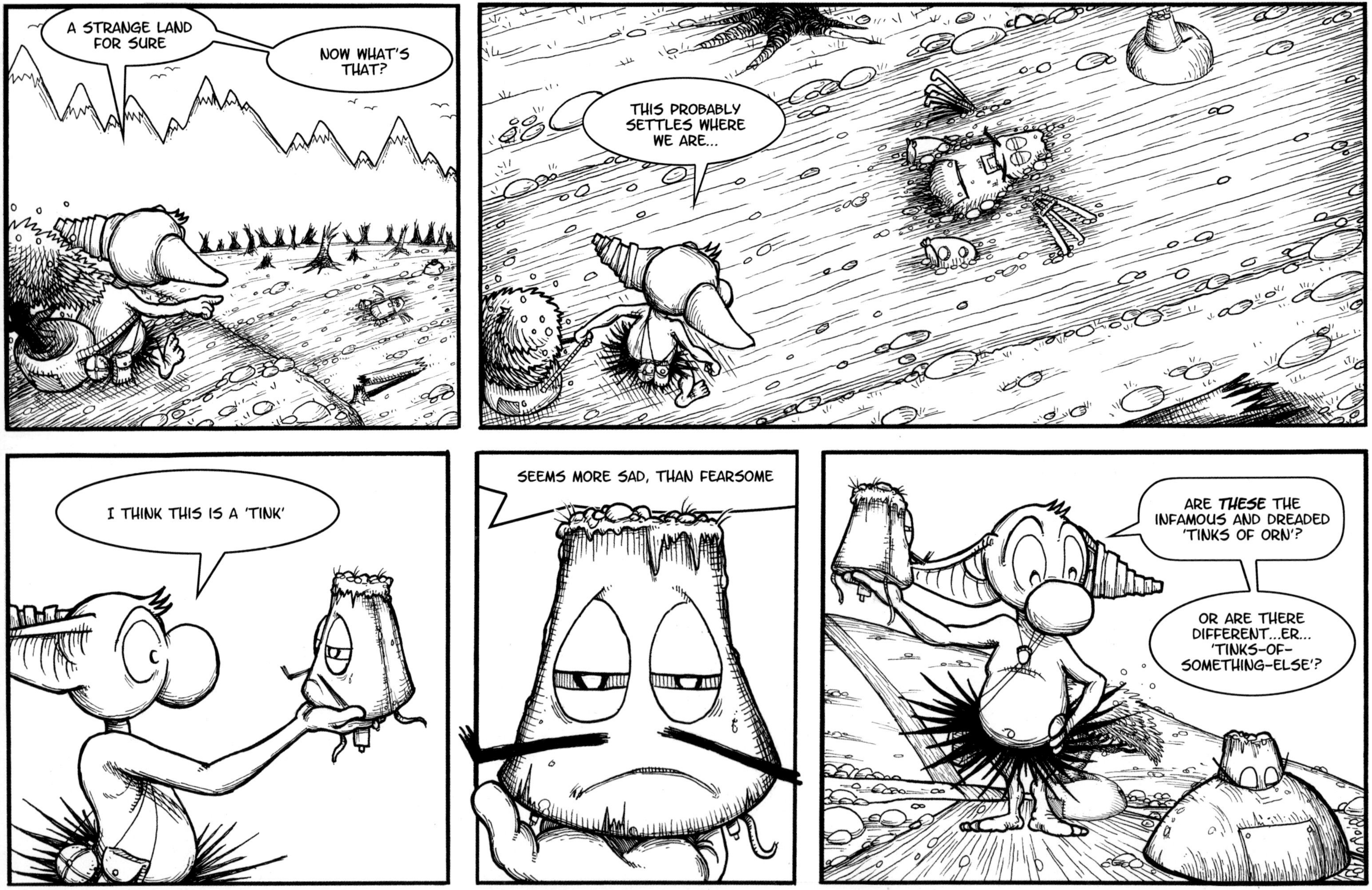
A STRANGE LAND FOR SURE
NOW WHAT'S THAT?
THIS PROBABLY SETTLES WHERE WE ARE...
I THINK THIS IS A 'TINK'
SEEMS MORE SAD, THAN FEARSOME
ARE *THESE* THE INFAMOUS AND DREADED 'TINKS OF ORN'?
OR ARE THERE DIFFERENT...ER... 'TINKS-OF-SOMETHING-ELSE'?

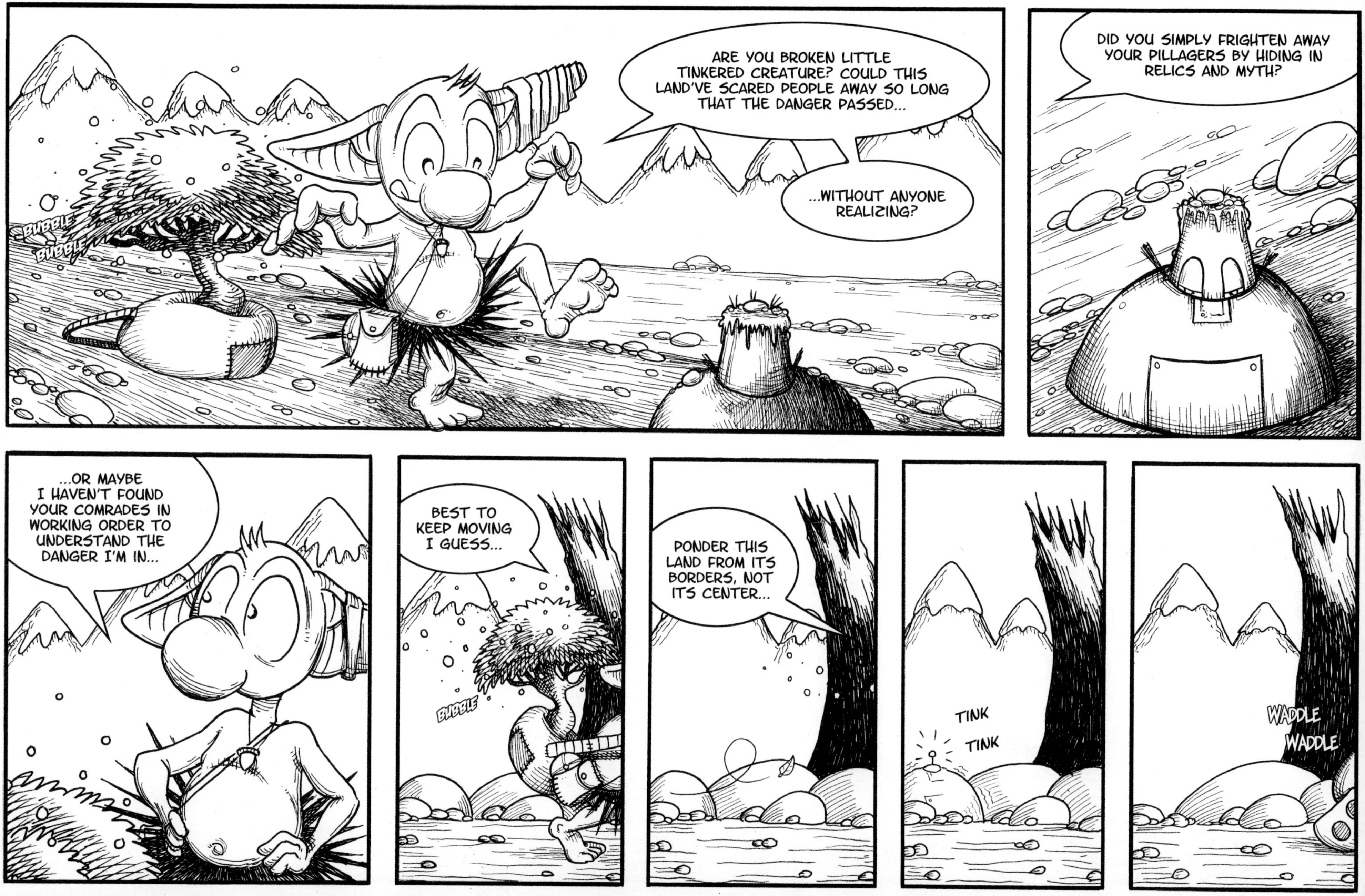
BUBBLE
BUBBLE
ARE YOU BROKEN LITTLE TINKERED CREATURE? COULD THIS LAND'VE SCARED PEOPLE AWAY SO LONG THAT THE DANGER PASSED...
...WITHOUT ANYONE REALIZING?
DID YOU SIMPLY FRIGHTEN AWAY YOUR PILLAGERS BY HIDING IN RELICS AND MYTH?
...OR MAYBE I HAVEN'T FOUND YOUR COMRADES IN WORKING ORDER TO UNDERSTAND THE DANGER I'M IN...
BEST TO KEEP MOVING I GUESS...
BUBBLE
PONDER THIS LAND FROM ITS BORDERS, NOT ITS CENTER...
TINK
TINK
WADDLE
WADDLE

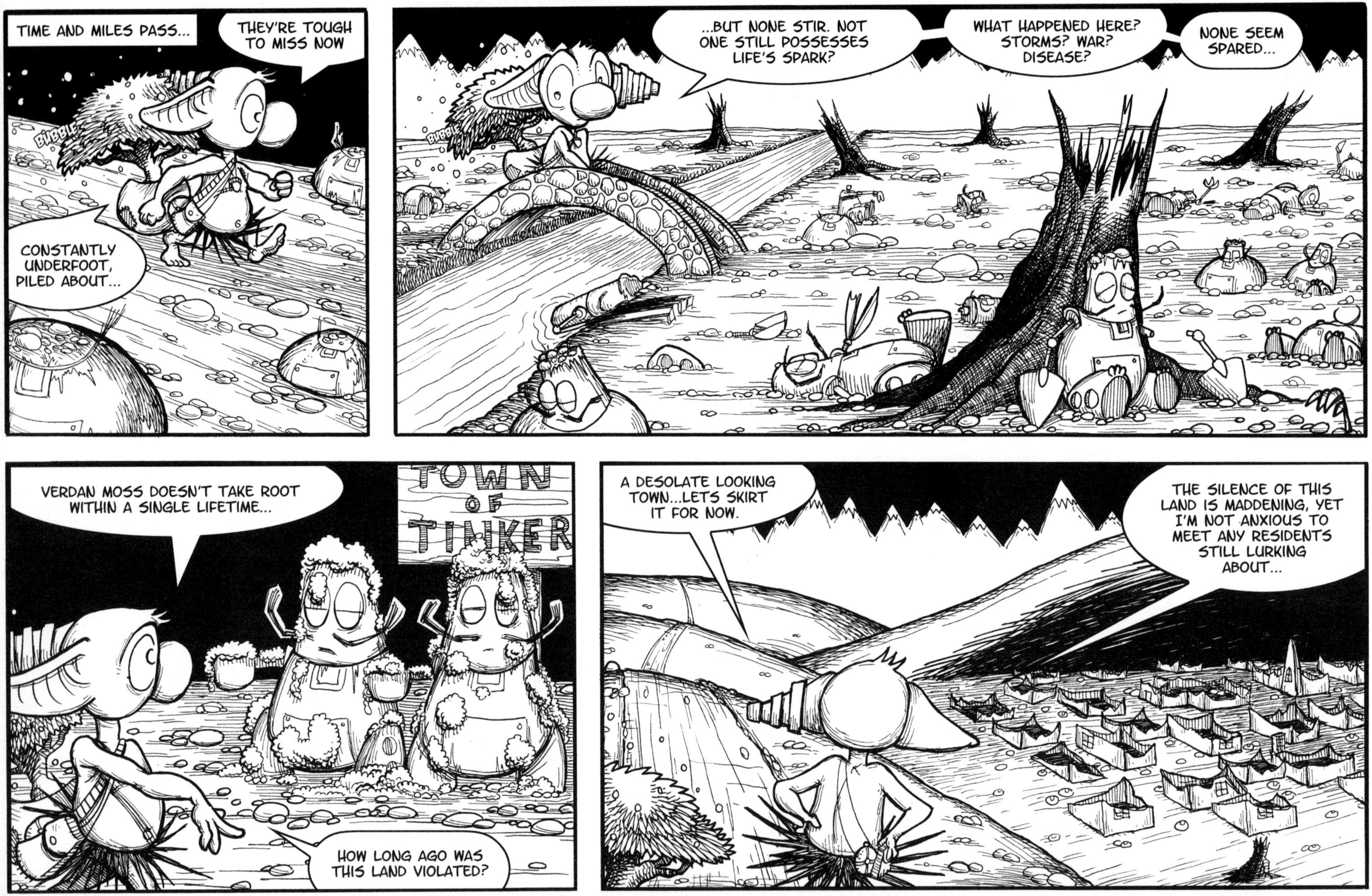
TIME AND MILES PASS...
THEY'RE TOUGH TO MISS NOW
BUBBLE
CONSTANTLY UNDERFOOT, PILED ABOUT...
BUBBLE
...BUT NONE STIR. NOT ONE STILL POSSESSES LIFE'S SPARK?
WHAT HAPPENED HERE? STORMS? WAR? DISEASE?
NONE SEEM SPARED...
VERDAN MOSS DOESN'T TAKE ROOT WITHIN A SINGLE LIFETIME...
TOWN OF TINKER
HOW LONG AGO WAS THIS LAND VIOLATED?
A DESOLATE LOOKING TOWN...LETS SKIRT IT FOR NOW.
THE SILENCE OF THIS LAND IS MADDENING, YET I'M NOT ANXIOUS TO MEET ANY RESIDENTS STILL LURKING ABOUT...

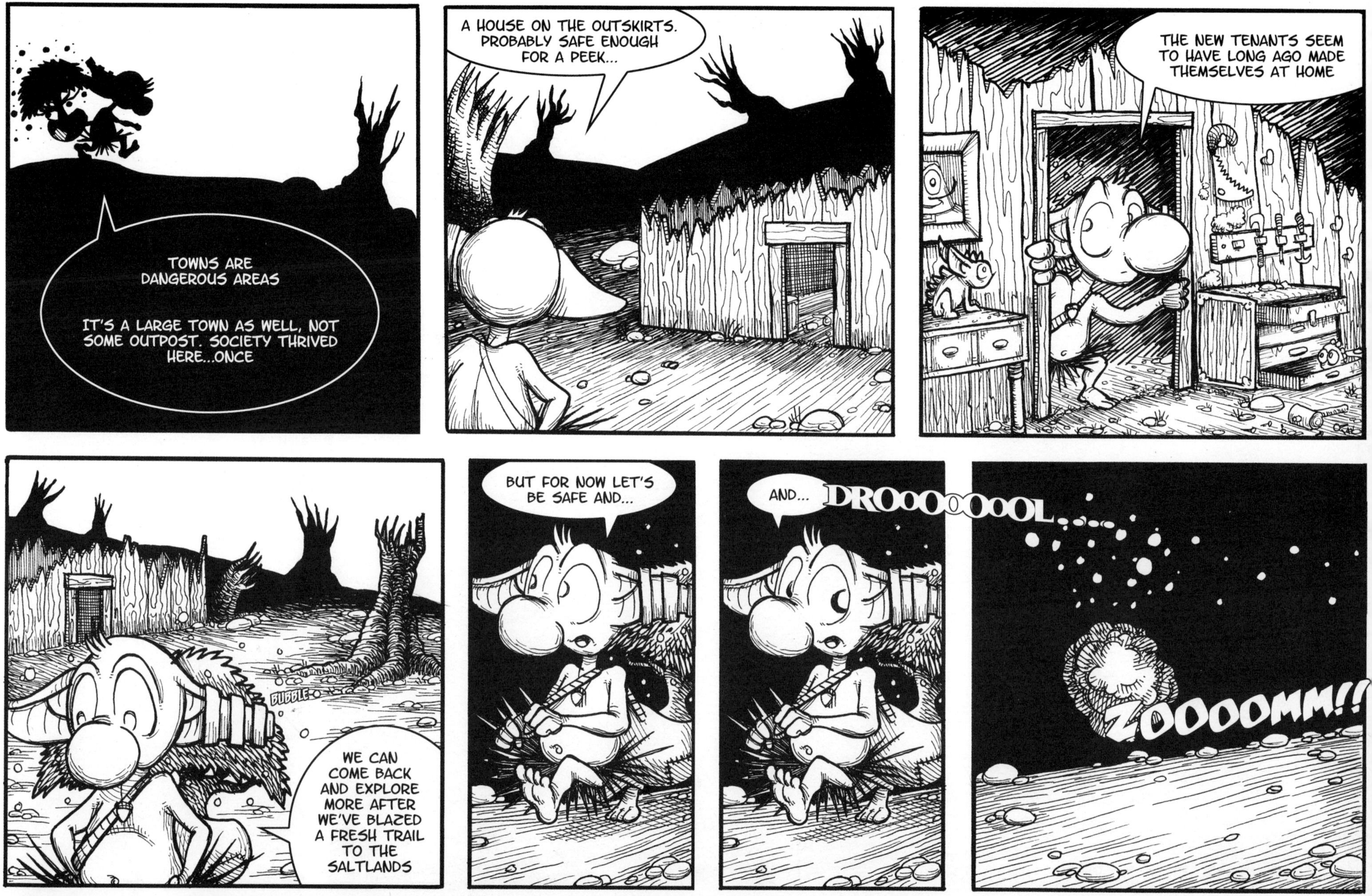

TOWNS ARE DANGEROUS AREAS
IT'S A LARGE TOWN AS WELL, NOT SOME OUTPOST. SOCIETY THRIVED HERE...ONCE
A HOUSE ON THE OUTSKIRTS. PROBABLY SAFE ENOUGH FOR A PEEK...
THE NEW TENANTS SEEM TO HAVE LONG AGO MADE THEMSELVES AT HOME
BUBBLE
WE CAN COME BACK AND EXPLORE MORE AFTER WE'VE BLAZED A FRESH TRAIL TO THE SALTLANDS
BUT FOR NOW LET'S BE SAFE AND...
AND...
DROOOOOOOL.....
ZOOOOMM!!

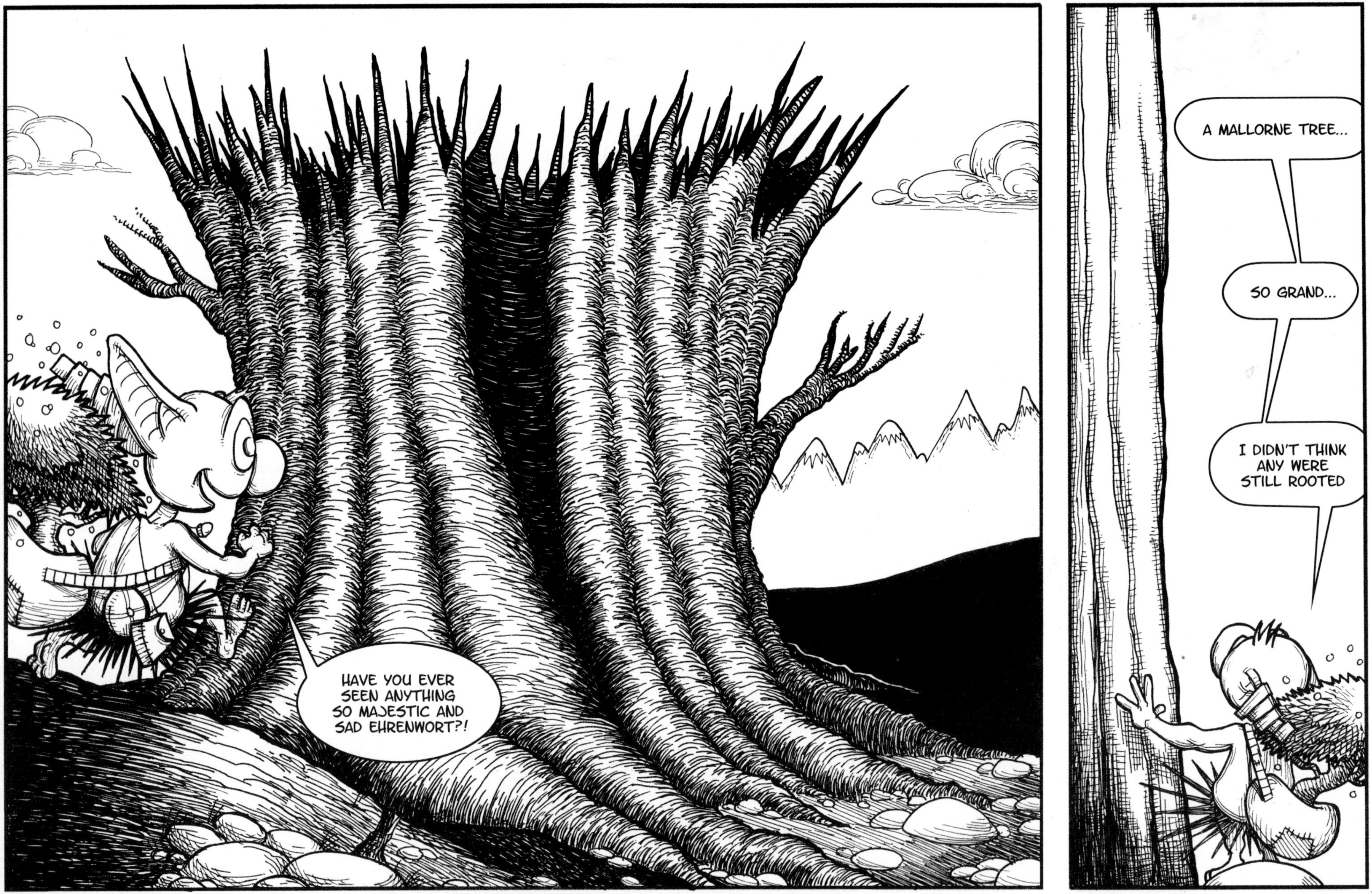

HAVE YOU EVER SEEN ANYTHING SO MAJESTIC AND SAD EHRENWORT?!
A MALLORNE TREE...
SO GRAND...
I DIDN'T THINK ANY WERE STILL ROOTED

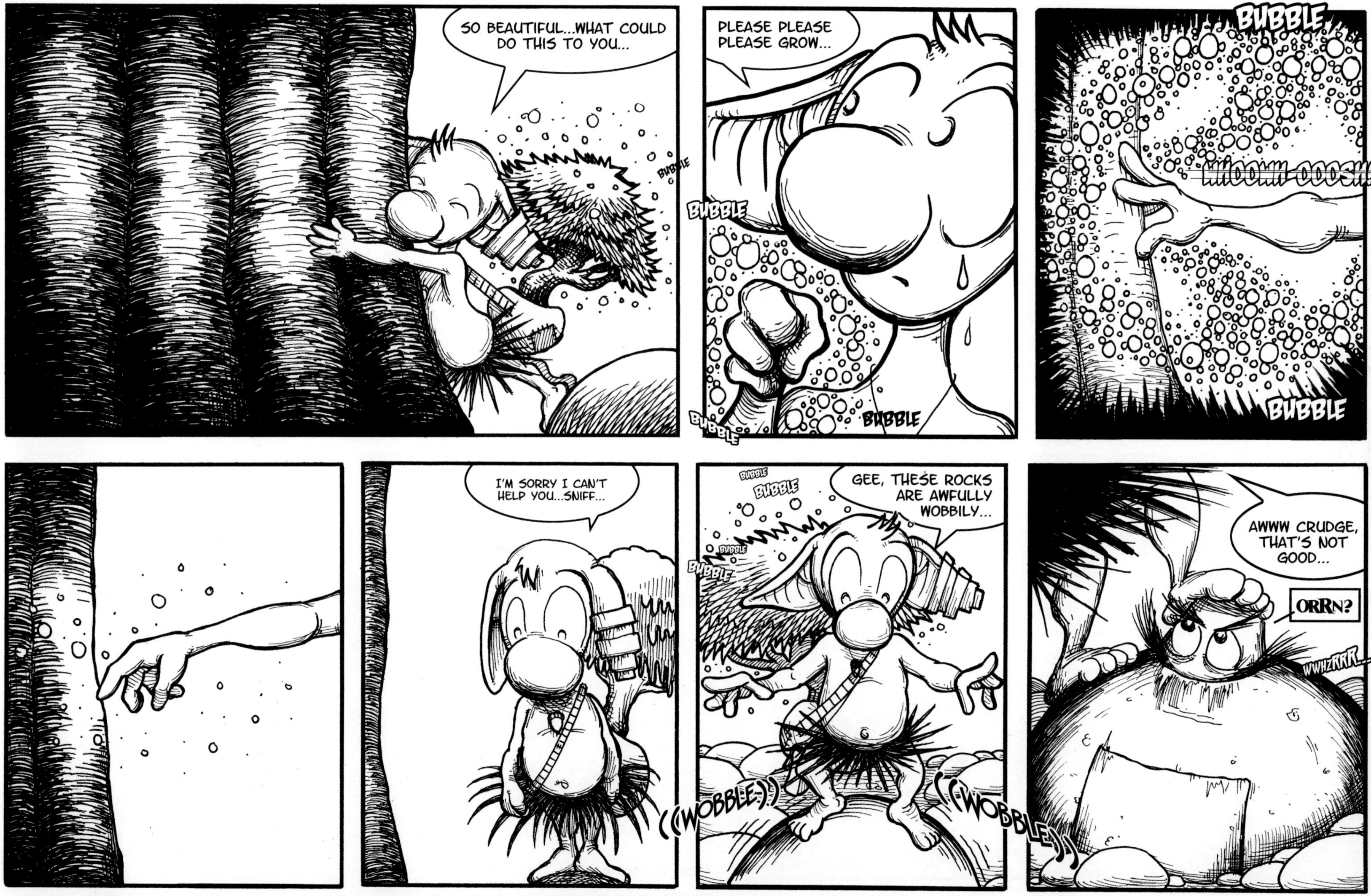
SO BEAUTIFUL...WHAT COULD DO THIS TO YOU...
BUBBLE
BUBBLE
PLEASE PLEASE PLEASE GROW...
BUBBLE
BUBBLE
BUBBLE
WHOOMM-OOOSH!
BUBBLE
I'M SORRY I CAN'T HELP YOU...SNIFF...
BUBBLE
BUBBLE
BUBBLE
BUBBLE
GEE, THESE ROCKS ARE AWFULLY WOBBILY...
((WOBBLE))
((WOBBLE))
AWWW CRUDGE, THAT'S NOT GOOD...
ORRN?
WWHZRRR...

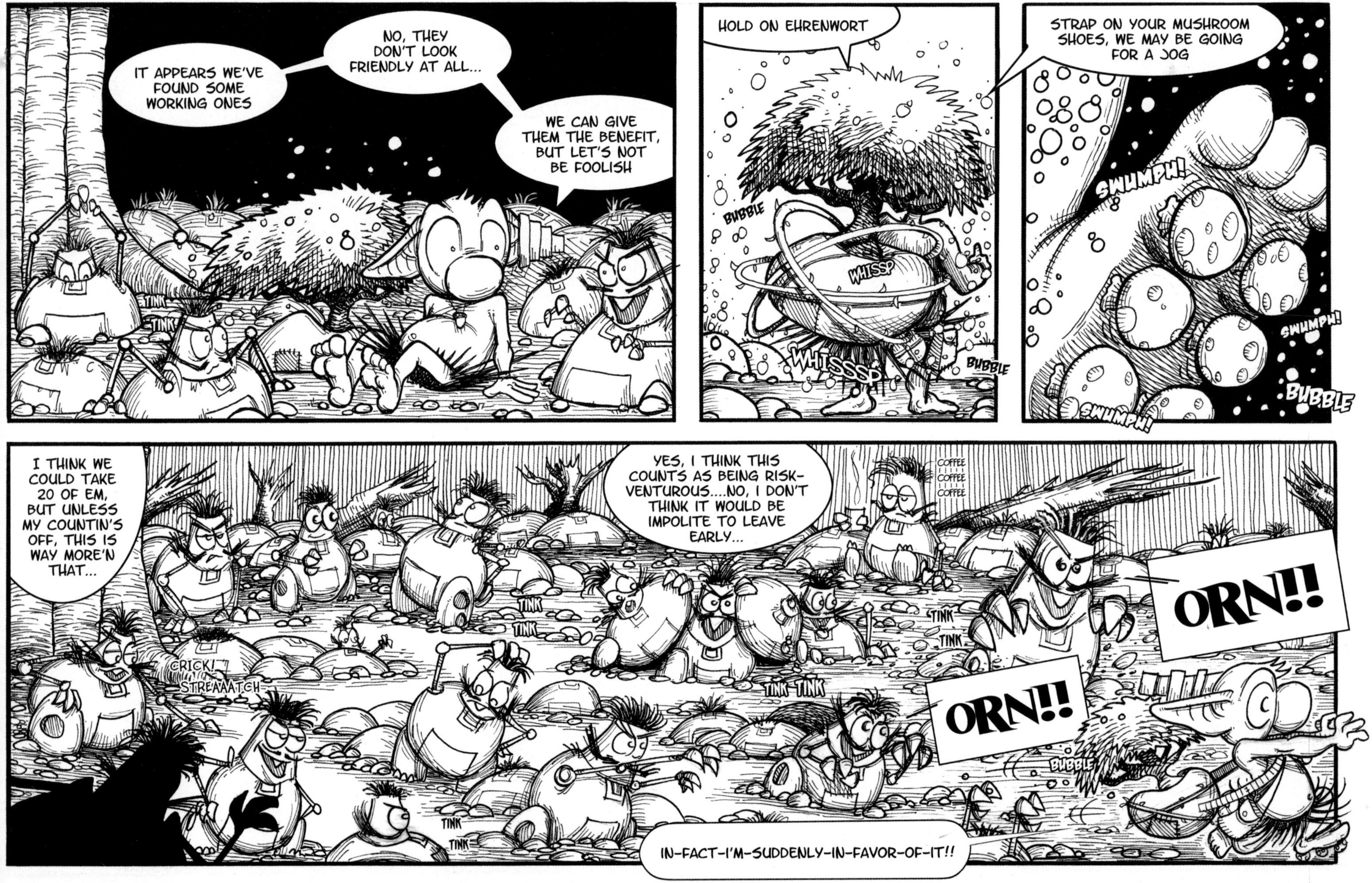

IT APPEARS WE'VE FOUND SOME WORKING ONES
NO, THEY DON'T LOOK FRIENDLY AT ALL...
WE CAN GIVE THEM THE BENEFIT, BUT LET'S NOT BE FOOLISH
TINK
TINK
HOLD ON EHRENWORT
BUBBLE
WHISSP
WHISSSP
BUBBLE
STRAP ON YOUR MUSHROOM SHOES, WE MAY BE GOING FOR A JOG
SWUMPH!
SWUMPH!
BUBBLE
SWUMPH!
I THINK WE COULD TAKE 20 OF EM, BUT UNLESS MY COUNTIN'S OFF, THIS IS WAY MORE'N THAT...
YES, I THINK THIS COUNTS AS BEING RISK-VENTUROUS....NO, I DON'T THINK IT WOULD BE IMPOLITE TO LEAVE EARLY...
COFFEE
COFFEE
COFFEE
TINK
TINK
TINK
TINK
CRICK!
STREAAATCH
TINK TINK
ORN!!
ORN!!
BUBBLE
TINK
TINK
IN-FACT-I'M-SUDDENLY-IN-FAVOR-OF-IT!!

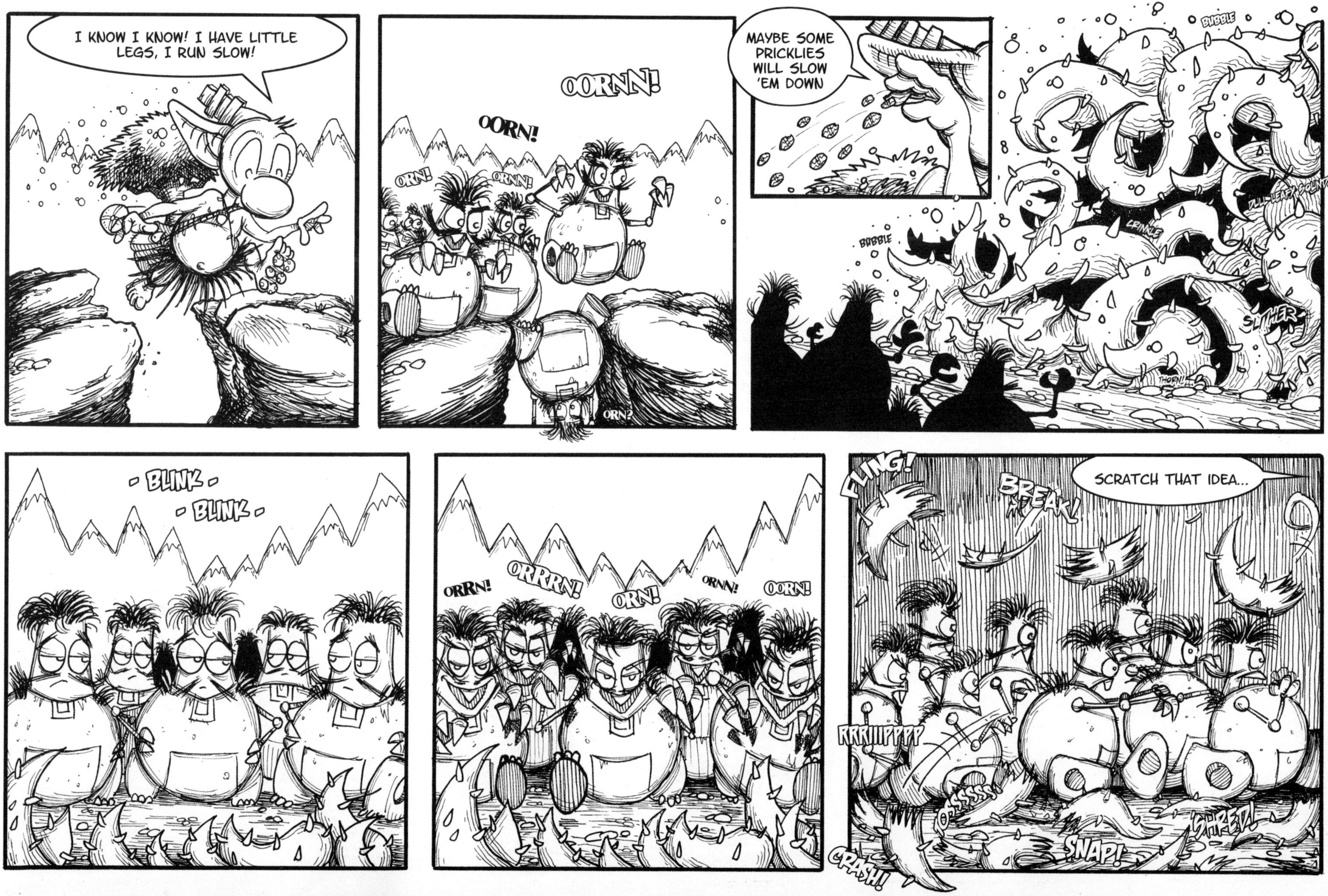

I KNOW I KNOW! I HAVE LITTLE LEGS, I RUN SLOW!
OORNN!
OORN!
ORN!
OORNN!
ORN?
MAYBE SOME PRICKLIES WILL SLOW 'EM DOWN
BUBBLE
DULL LEAFY SOUND!
CRINKLE
BUBBLE
SLYTHER
THORN!
- BLINK -
- BLINK -
ORRN!
ORRRRN!
ORN!
ORNN!
OORN!
FLING!
BREAK!
SCRATCH THAT IDEA...
RRRIIIPPPP
CRASH!
SNAP!
SHRED!

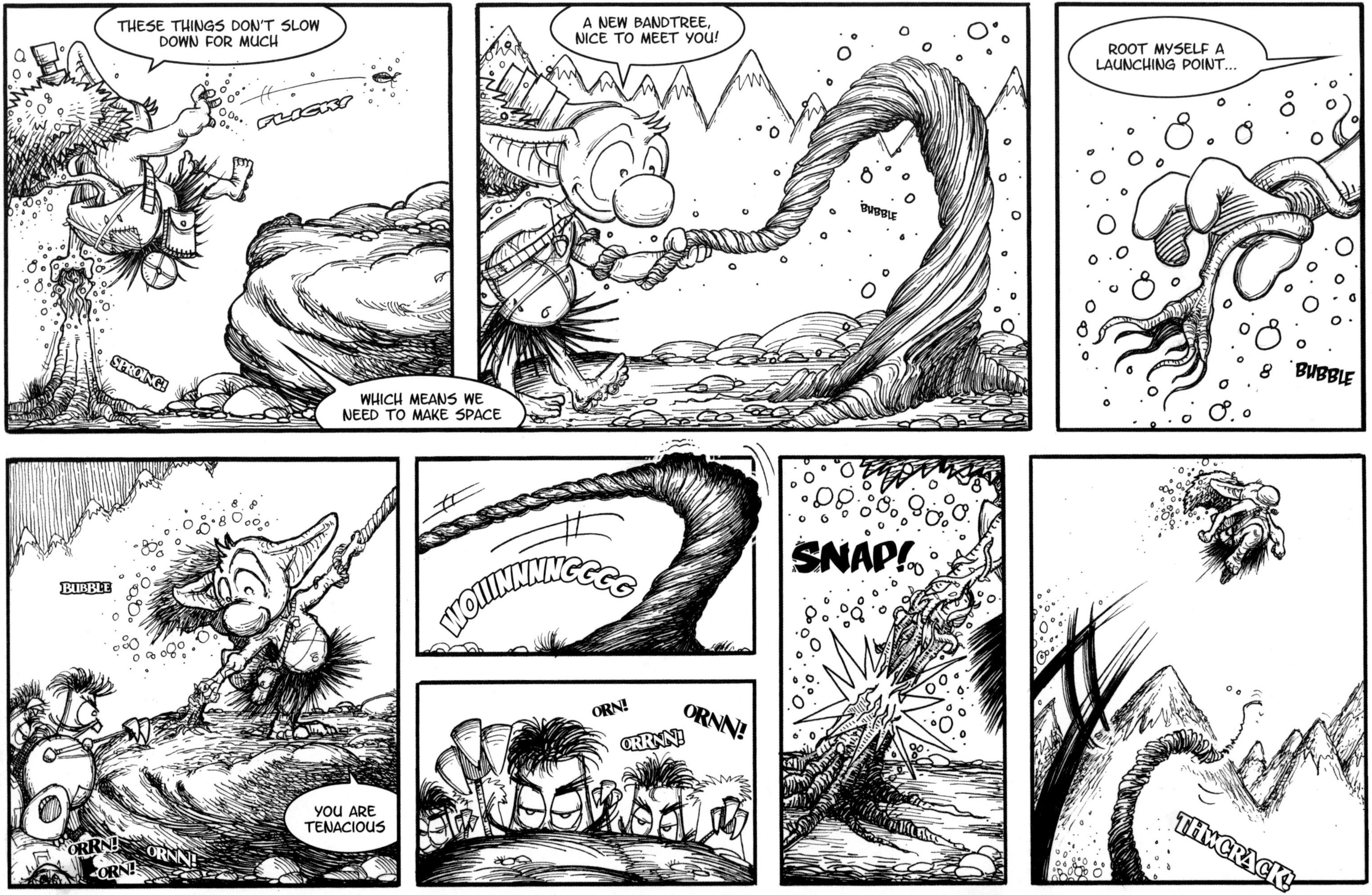
THESE THINGS DON'T SLOW DOWN FOR MUCH
FLICK!
SPRONG!
WHICH MEANS WE NEED TO MAKE SPACE
A NEW BANDTREE, NICE TO MEET YOU!
BUBBLE
ROOT MYSELF A LAUNCHING POINT...
BUBBLE
BUBBLE
YOU ARE TENACIOUS
ORRN!
ORN!
ORNN!
WOIIINNNNGGGG
ORN!
ORRNN!
ORNN!
SNAP!
THWCRACK!

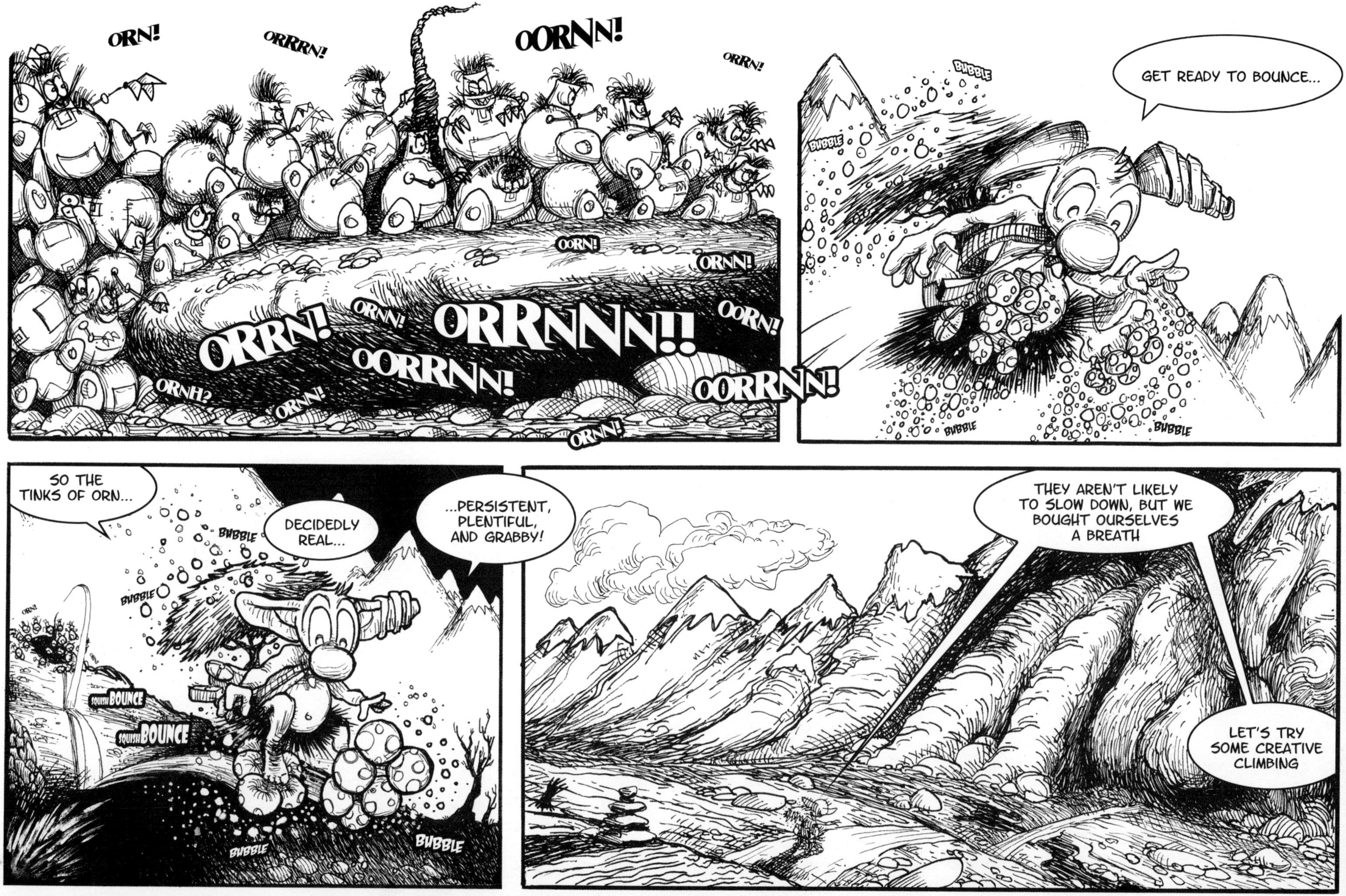
ORN!
ORRRN!
OORNN!
ORRN!
OORN!
ORNN!
ORRN!
ORNN!
ORRRNNN!!
OORN!
OORRRNN!
OORRNN!
ORNH?
ORNN!
ORNN!
BUBBLE
BUBBLE
GET READY TO BOUNCE...
BUBBLE
BUBBLE
SO THE TINKS OF ORN...
DECIDEDLY REAL...
...PERSISTENT, PLENTIFUL, AND GRABBY!
BUBBLE
BUBBLE
SQUISH BOUNCE
SQUISH BOUNCE
BUBBLE
BUBBLE
THEY AREN'T LIKELY TO SLOW DOWN, BUT WE BOUGHT OURSELVES A BREATH
LET'S TRY SOME CREATIVE CLIMBING

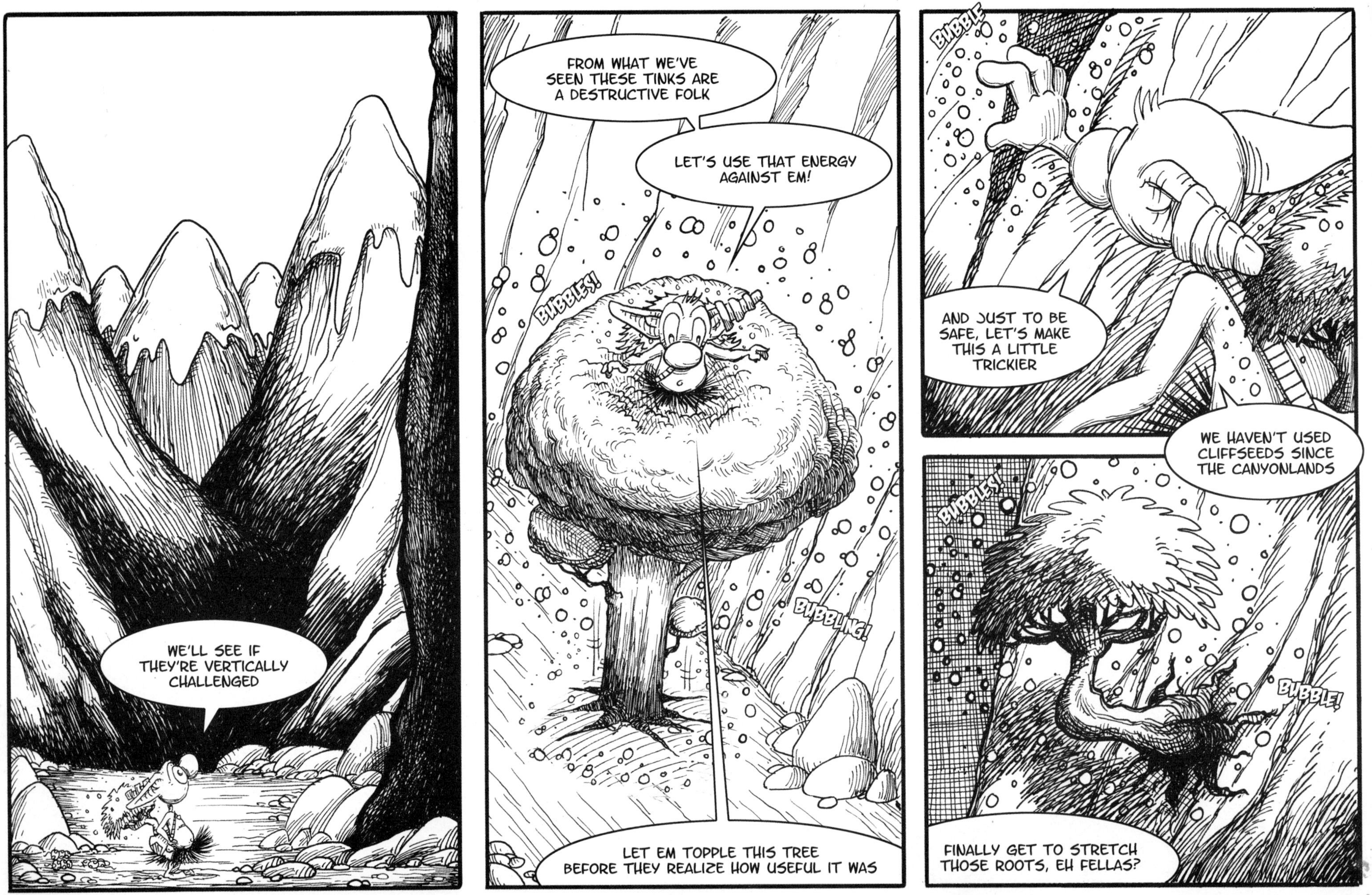
WE'LL SEE IF THEY'RE VERTICALLY CHALLENGED
FROM WHAT WE'VE SEEN THESE TINKS ARE A DESTRUCTIVE FOLK
LET'S USE THAT ENERGY AGAINST EM!
BUBBLES!
BUBBLING!
LET EM TOPPLE THIS TREE BEFORE THEY REALIZE HOW USEFUL IT WAS
BUBBLE
AND JUST TO BE SAFE, LET'S MAKE THIS A LITTLE TRICKIER
WE HAVEN'T USED CLIFFSEEDS SINCE THE CANYONLANDS
BUBBLES!
BUBBLE!
FINALLY GET TO STRETCH THOSE ROOTS, EH FELLAS?

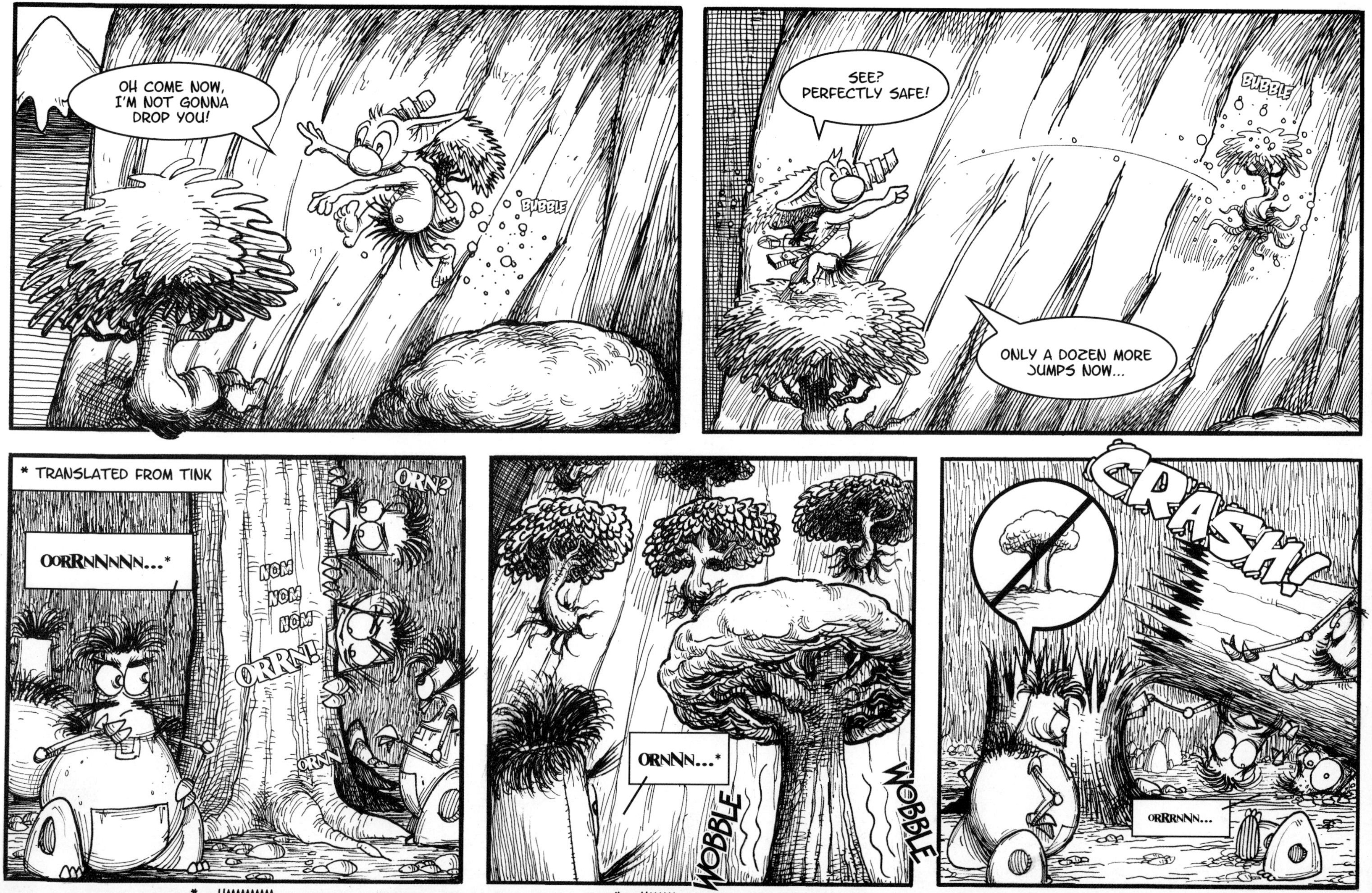
OH COME NOW, I'M NOT GONNA DROP YOU!
BUBBLE
SEE? PERFECTLY SAFE!
BUBBLE
ONLY A DOZEN MORE JUMPS NOW...
* TRANSLATED FROM TINK
OORRNNNNN...*
ORN?
NOM NOM NOM
ORRN!
ORN
ORNNN...*
WOBBLE
WOBBLE
CRASH!
ORRRNNN...

* - HMMMMM...

* - HMMM...

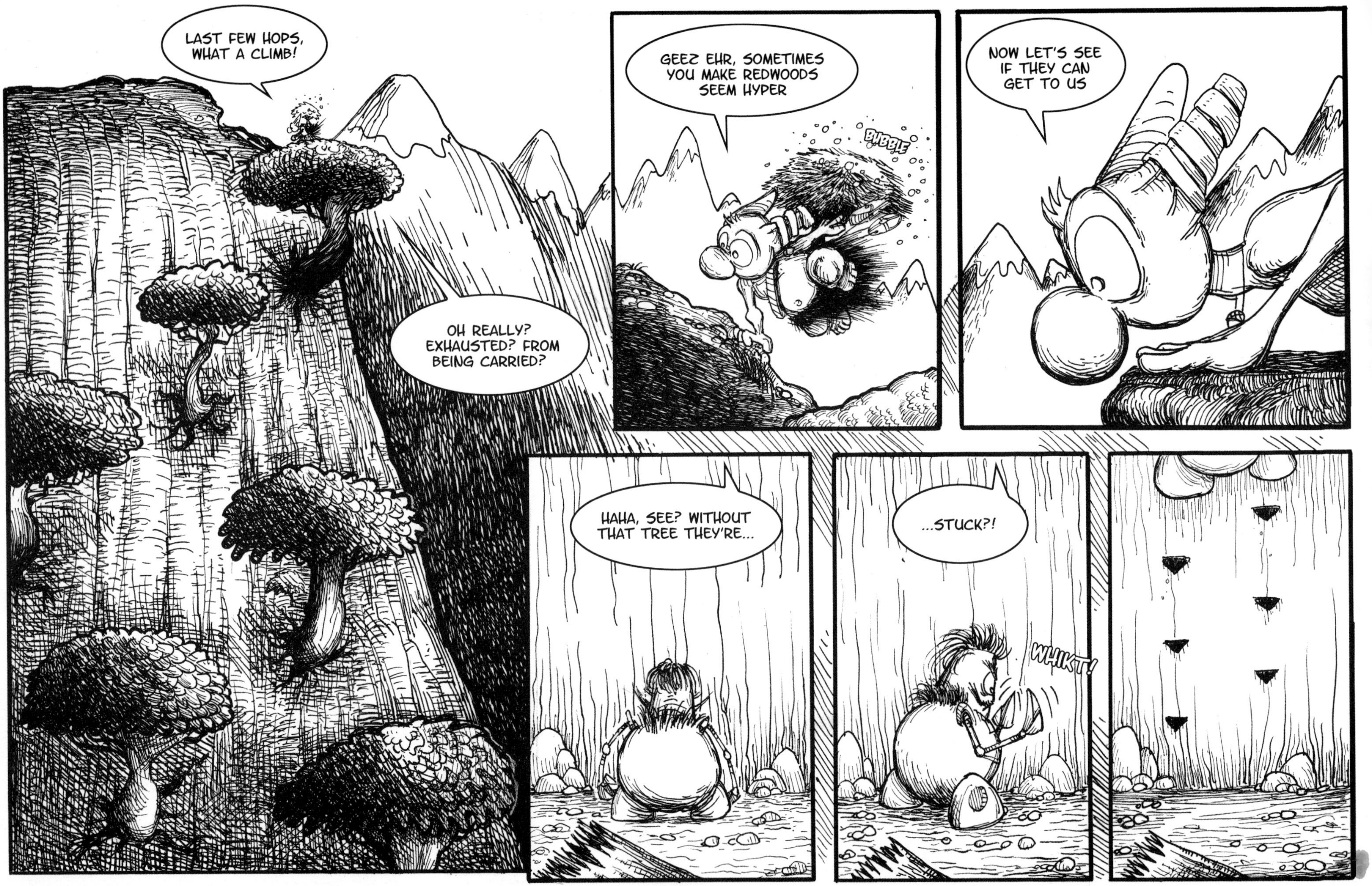
LAST FEW HOPS, WHAT A CLIMB!
OH REALLY? EXHAUSTED? FROM BEING CARRIED?
GEEZ EHR, SOMETIMES YOU MAKE REDWOODS SEEM HYPER
BUBBLE
NOW LET'S SEE IF THEY CAN GET TO US
HAHA, SEE? WITHOUT THAT TREE THEY'RE...
...STUCK?!
WHIKT!

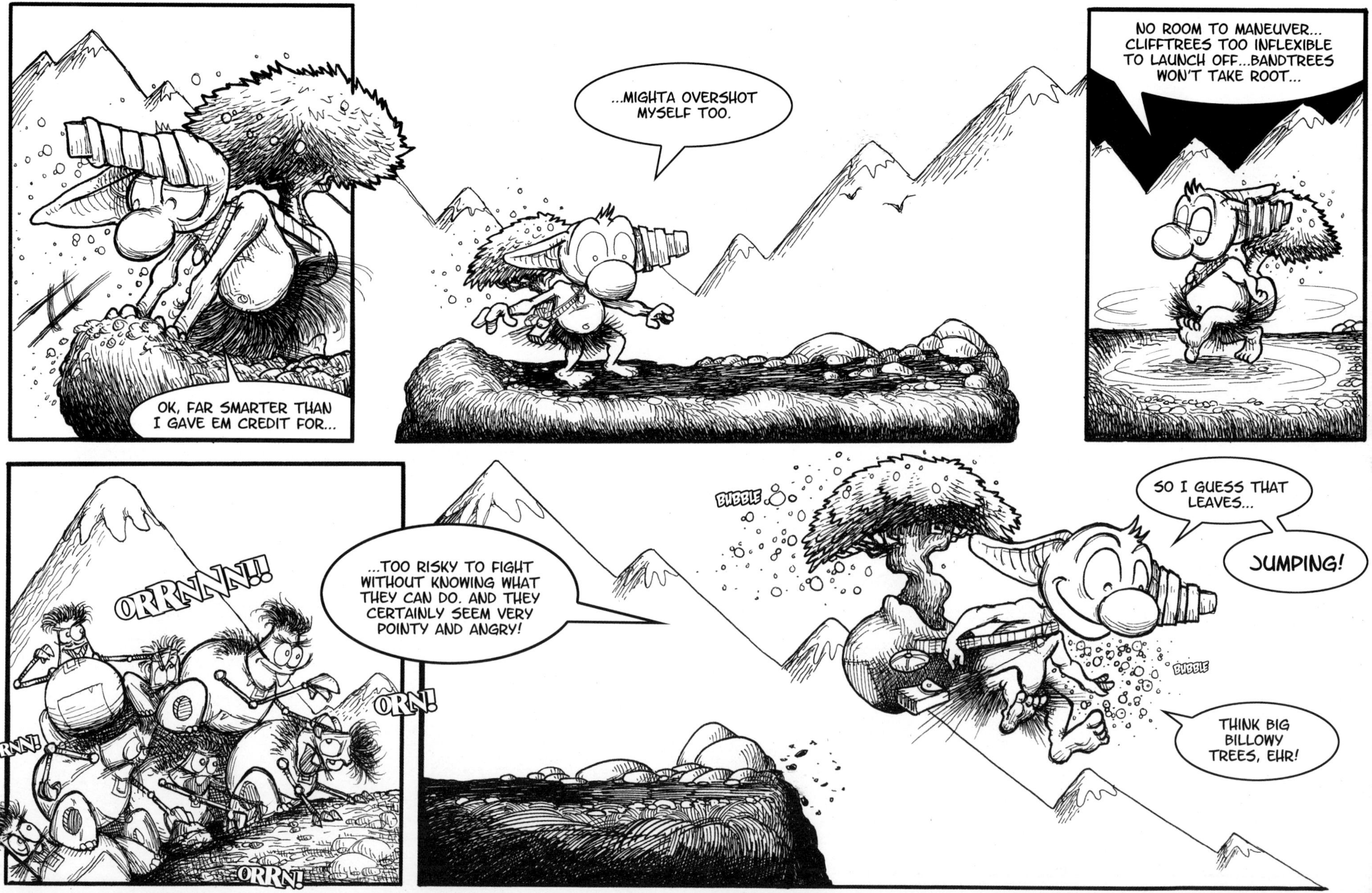

OK, FAR SMARTER THAN I GAVE EM CREDIT FOR...
...MIGHTA OVERSHOT MYSELF TOO.
NO ROOM TO MANEUVER... CLIFFTREES TOO INFLEXIBLE TO LAUNCH OFF...BANDTREES WON'T TAKE ROOT...
ORRNNNN!!
ORN!
ORRNN!
ORRN!
...TOO RISKY TO FIGHT WITHOUT KNOWING WHAT THEY CAN DO. AND THEY CERTAINLY SEEM VERY POINTY AND ANGRY!
BUBBLE
SO I GUESS THAT LEAVES...
JUMPING!
BUBBLE
THINK BIG BILLOWY TREES, EHR!

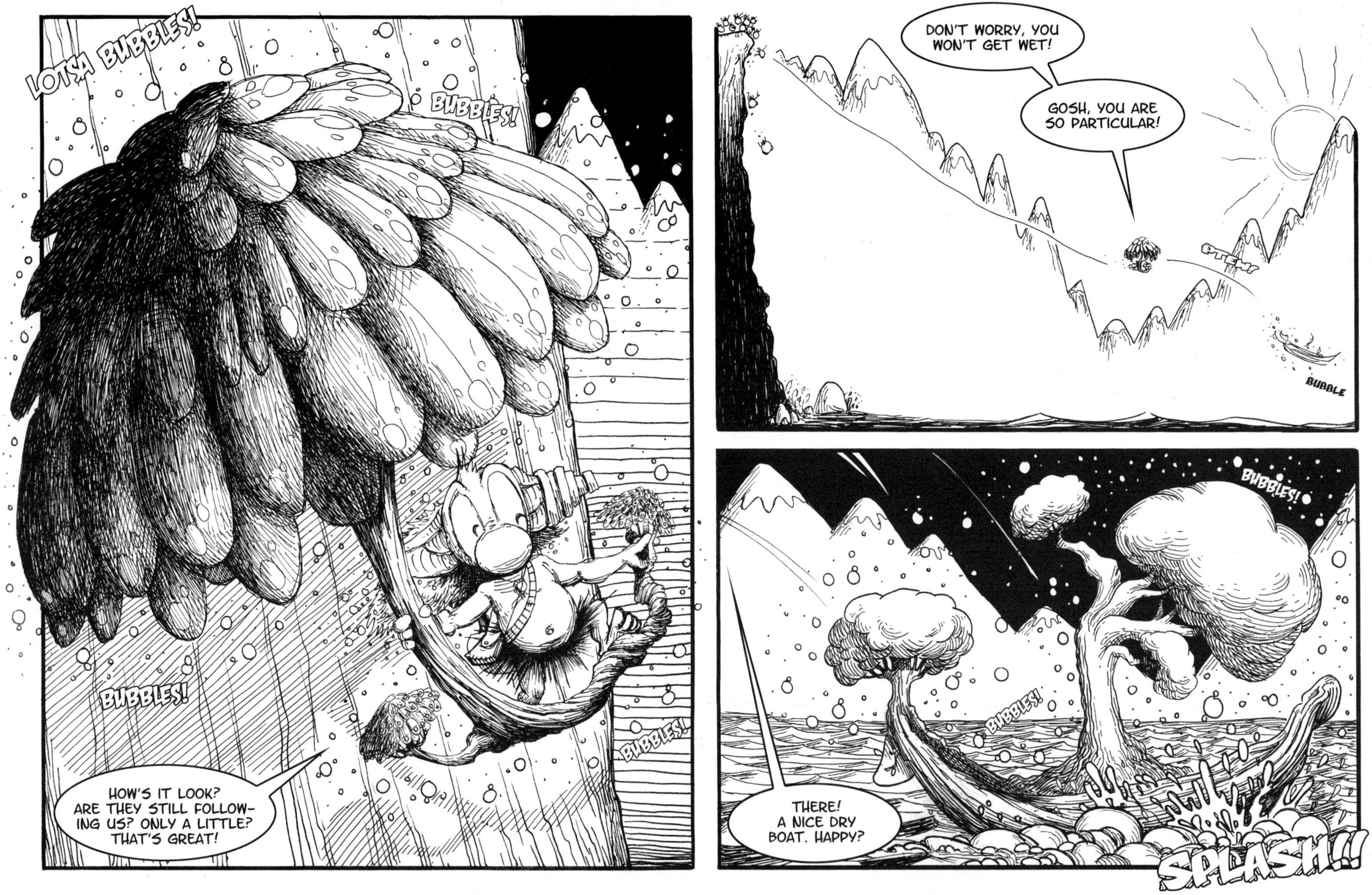
LOTSA BUBBLES!
BUBBLES!
BUBBLES!
BUBBLES!
HOW'S IT LOOK? ARE THEY STILL FOLLOW-ING US? ONLY A LITTLE? THAT'S GREAT!
DON'T WORRY, YOU WON'T GET WET!
GOSH, YOU ARE SO PARTICULAR!
BUBBLE
BUBBLES!
BUBBLES!
THERE! A NICE DRY BOAT. HAPPY?
SPLASH!!

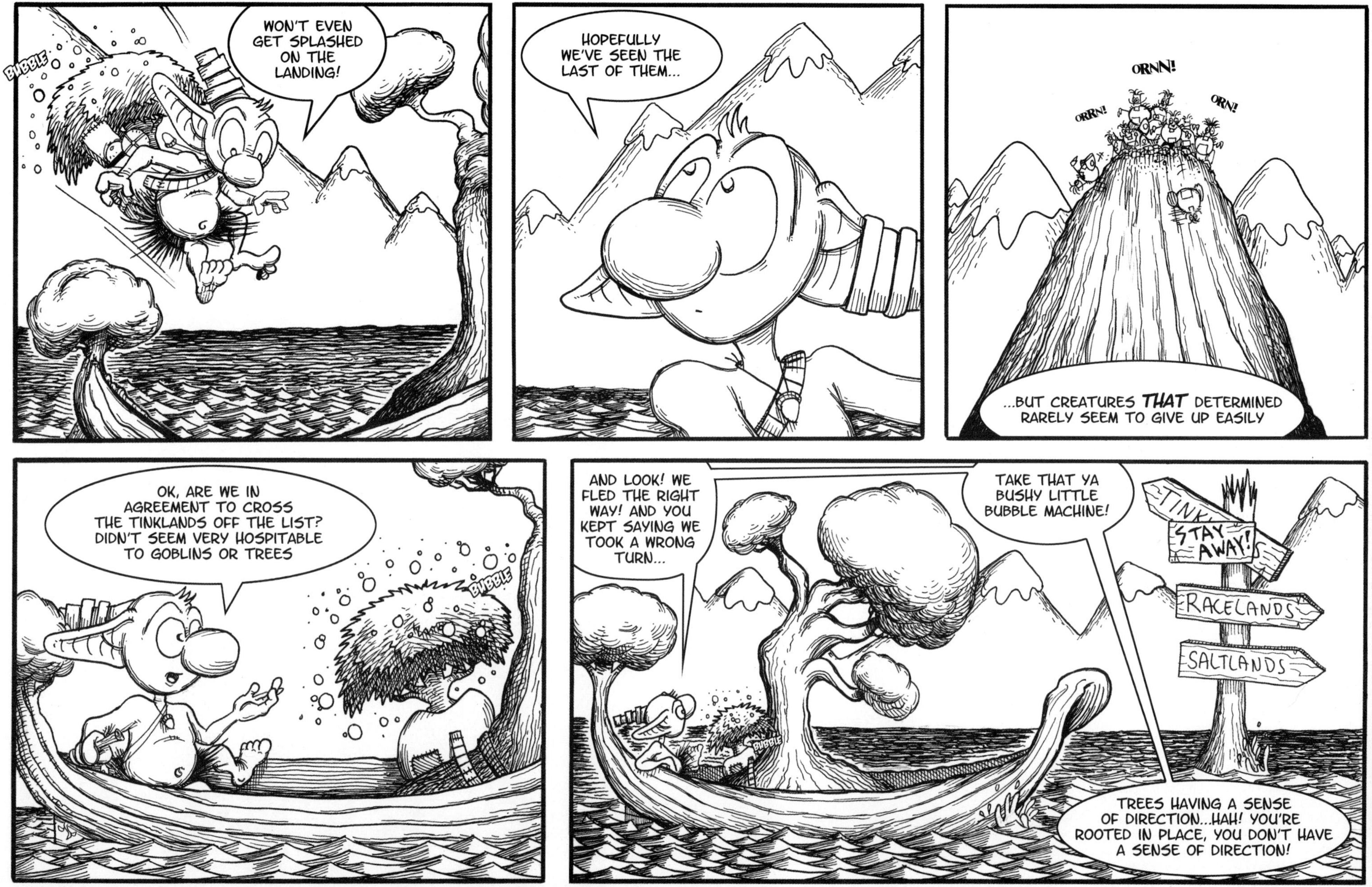
BUBBLE
WON'T EVEN GET SPLASHED ON THE LANDING!
HOPEFULLY WE'VE SEEN THE LAST OF THEM...
ORRN!
ORNN!
ORN!
...BUT CREATURES THAT DETERMINED RARELY SEEM TO GIVE UP EASILY
OK, ARE WE IN AGREEMENT TO CROSS THE TINKLANDS OFF THE LIST? DIDN'T SEEM VERY HOSPITABLE TO GOBLINS OR TREES
BUBBLE
AND LOOK! WE FLED THE RIGHT WAY! AND YOU KEPT SAYING WE TOOK A WRONG TURN...
TAKE THAT YA BUSHY LITTLE BUBBLE MACHINE!
STAY AWAY!
RACELANDS
SALTLANDS
BUBBLE
TREES HAVING A SENSE OF DIRECTION...HAH! YOU'RE ROOTED IN PLACE, YOU DON'T HAVE A SENSE OF DIRECTION!

HOWDY!

THANKS FOR PICKING UP THE BOOK!
I HOPE YOU ENJOY IT!

THE COMIC YOU'RE READING IS
BOOK 1 IN A 7-ISSUE SERIES THAT
TELLS THE STORY OF THE FINAL
LANDS VISITED BY THE LONG
JOURNEYING TREE GOBLIN SHAMAN
FARLAINE AND HIS BEST TREE EHRENWORT.

THE FIRST 3 BOOKS WERE WRITTEN AND DRAWN OVER A
9-MONTH STRETCH OF AVOIDING THE CUBICLE WORLD. I'VE SINCE
HAD TO GO BACK AND NOW FIT WRITING AND DRAWING IN ON
NIGHTS AND WEEKENDS.

THIS MEANS IT'S SLOWER TO COME OUT. MY LIKELY SCHEDULE
SEEMS TO BE 1 BOOK/YEAR.

BUT I'M TRYING TO PUT THE MOST I CAN INTO THAT ONE BOOK!

I HOPE YOU STICK AROUND FOR THE RIDE. IT ONLY GETS BETTER!

-J

FARLAINE THE GOBLIN. Book 1, THE TINKLANDS, June 2015 THIRD PRINTING
Published by Studio Farlaine, goblin@farlaine.com
ISBN 978-0-9890058-0-7

CONTACT THE AUTHOR
goblin@farlaine.com

READ ALL OF
FARLAINE'S ADVENTURES!

BOOK 1: FARLAINE IN THE TINKLANDS
BOOK 2: FARLAINE IN THE SALTLANDS
BOOK 3: FARLAINE IN THE RACELANDS
BOOK 4: FARLAINE IN THE TWISTLANDS
BOOK 5: FARLAINE IN THE VAULTLANDS
BOOK 6: FARLAINE IN THE WINGLANDS
BOOK 7: ?

FARLAINE.COM
FACEBOOK.COM/FARLAINETHEGOBLIN

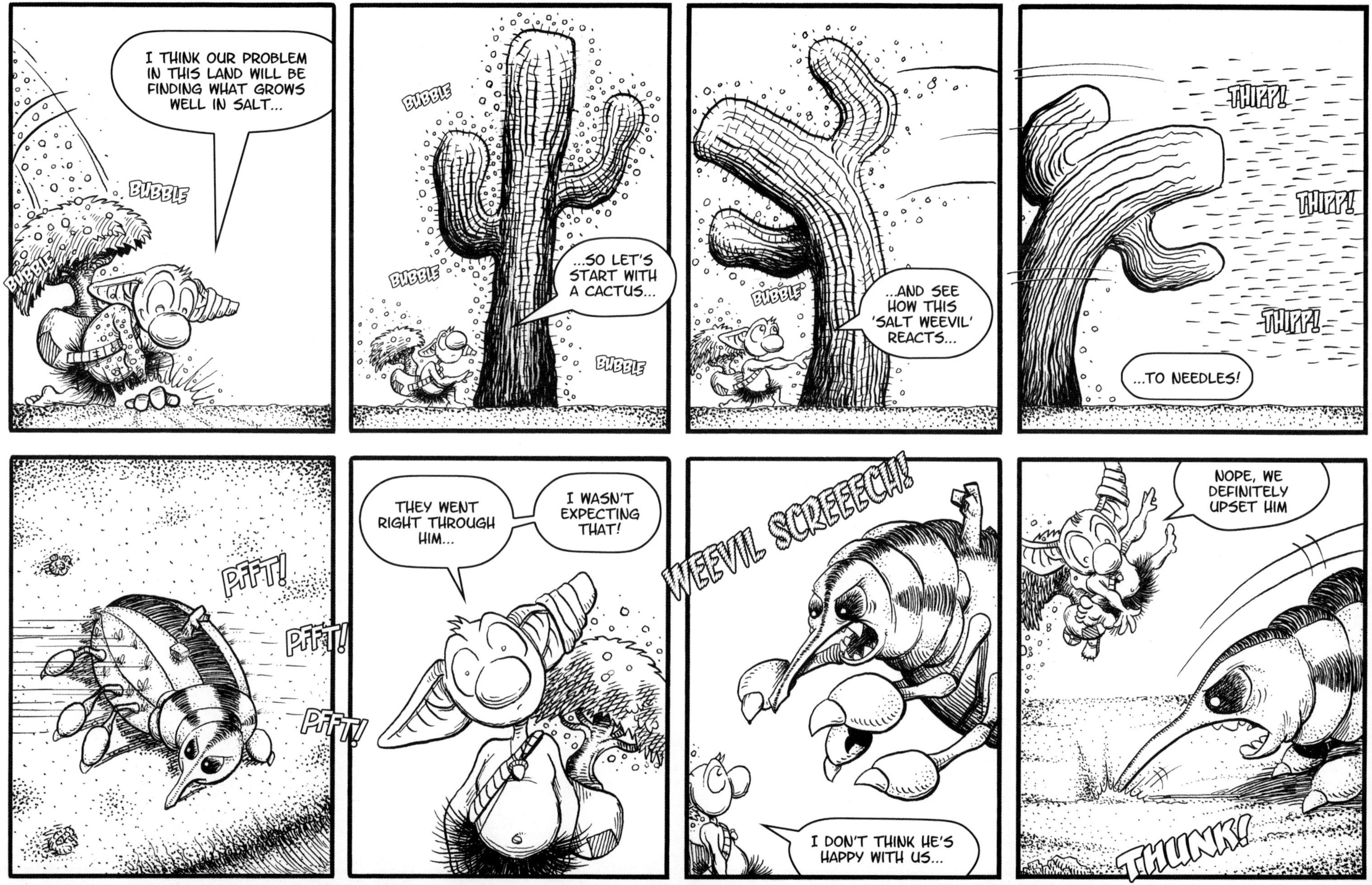
I THINK OUR PROBLEM IN THIS LAND WILL BE FINDING WHAT GROWS WELL IN SALT...
BUBBLE
BUBBLE
BUBBLE
BUBBLE
...SO LET'S START WITH A CACTUS...
BUBBLE
BUBBLE
...AND SEE HOW THIS 'SALT WEEVIL' REACTS...
THIPP!
THIPP!
THIPP!
...TO NEEDLES!
PFFT!
PFFT!
PFFT!
THEY WENT RIGHT THROUGH HIM...
I WASN'T EXPECTING THAT!
WEEVIL SCREEECH!
I DON'T THINK HE'S HAPPY WITH US...
NOPE, WE DEFINITELY UPSET HIM
THUNK!

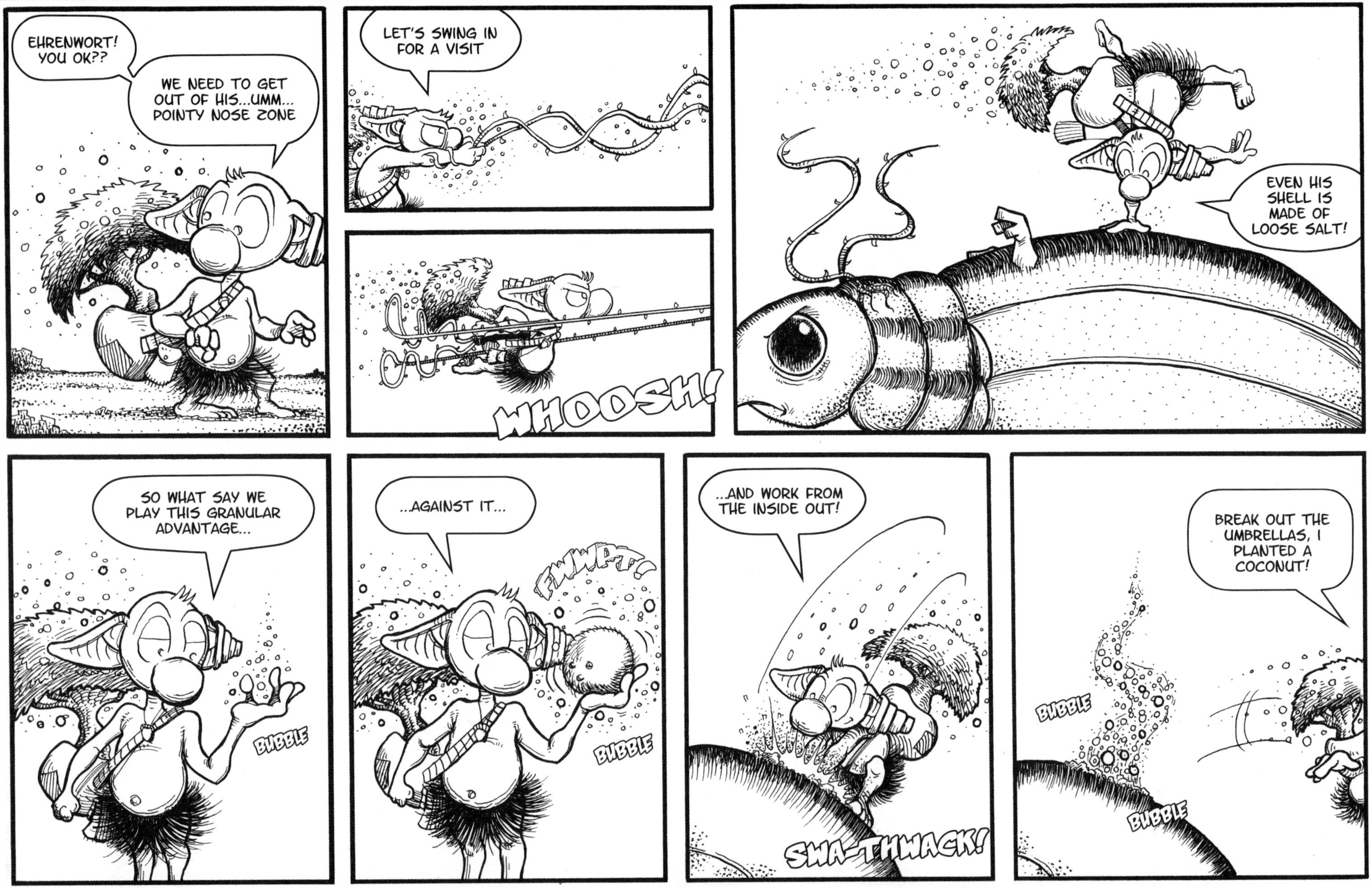
EHRENWORT! YOU OK??
WE NEED TO GET OUT OF HIS...UMM... POINTY NOSE ZONE
LET'S SWING IN FOR A VISIT
WHOOSH!
EVEN HIS SHELL IS MADE OF LOOSE SALT!
SO WHAT SAY WE PLAY THIS GRANULAR ADVANTAGE...
BUBBLE
...AGAINST IT...
FWWAT!
BUBBLE
...AND WORK FROM THE INSIDE OUT!
SWA-THWACK!
BREAK OUT THE UMBRELLAS, I PLANTED A COCONUT!
BUBBLE
BUBBLE

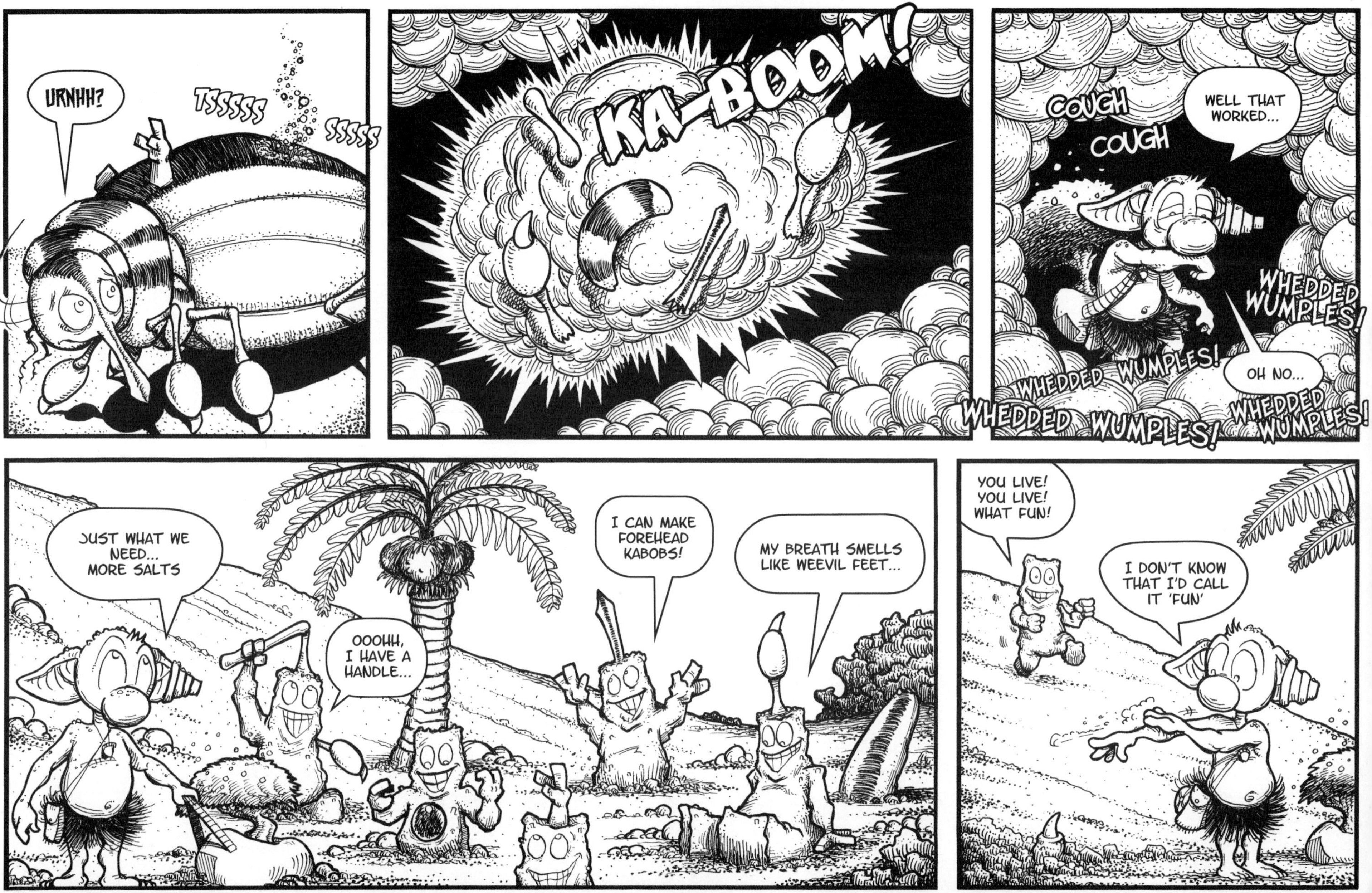
URNHH?
TSSSSS
SSSSS
KA-BOOM!
COUGH
COUGH
WELL THAT WORKED...
WHEDDED WUMPLES!
WHEDDED WUMPLES!
OH NO...
WHEDDED WUMPLES!
WHEDDED WUMPLES!
JUST WHAT WE NEED... MORE SALTS
OOOHH, I HAVE A HANDLE...
I CAN MAKE FOREHEAD KABOBS!
MY BREATH SMELLS LIKE WEEVIL FEET...
YOU LIVE! YOU LIVE! WHAT FUN!
I DON'T KNOW THAT I'D CALL IT 'FUN'

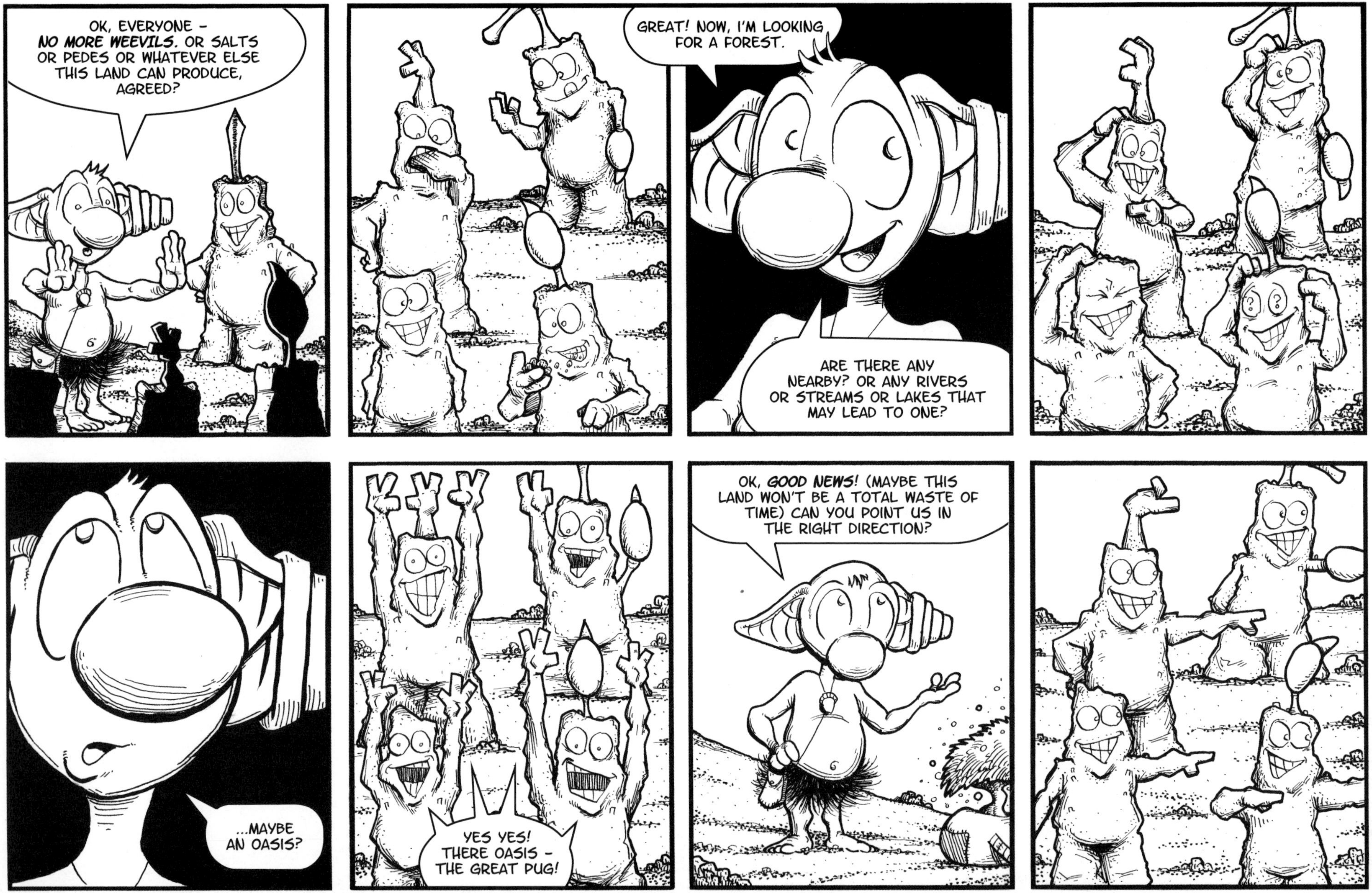
OK, EVERYONE - *NO MORE WEEVILS.* OR SALTS OR PEDES OR WHATEVER ELSE THIS LAND CAN PRODUCE, AGREED?
GREAT! NOW, I'M LOOKING FOR A FOREST.
ARE THERE ANY NEARBY? OR ANY RIVERS OR STREAMS OR LAKES THAT MAY LEAD TO ONE?
...MAYBE AN OASIS?
YES YES! THERE OASIS - THE GREAT PUG!
OK, *GOOD NEWS!* (MAYBE THIS LAND WON'T BE A TOTAL WASTE OF TIME) CAN YOU POINT US IN THE RIGHT DIRECTION?

END OF SNEAK PREVIEW!

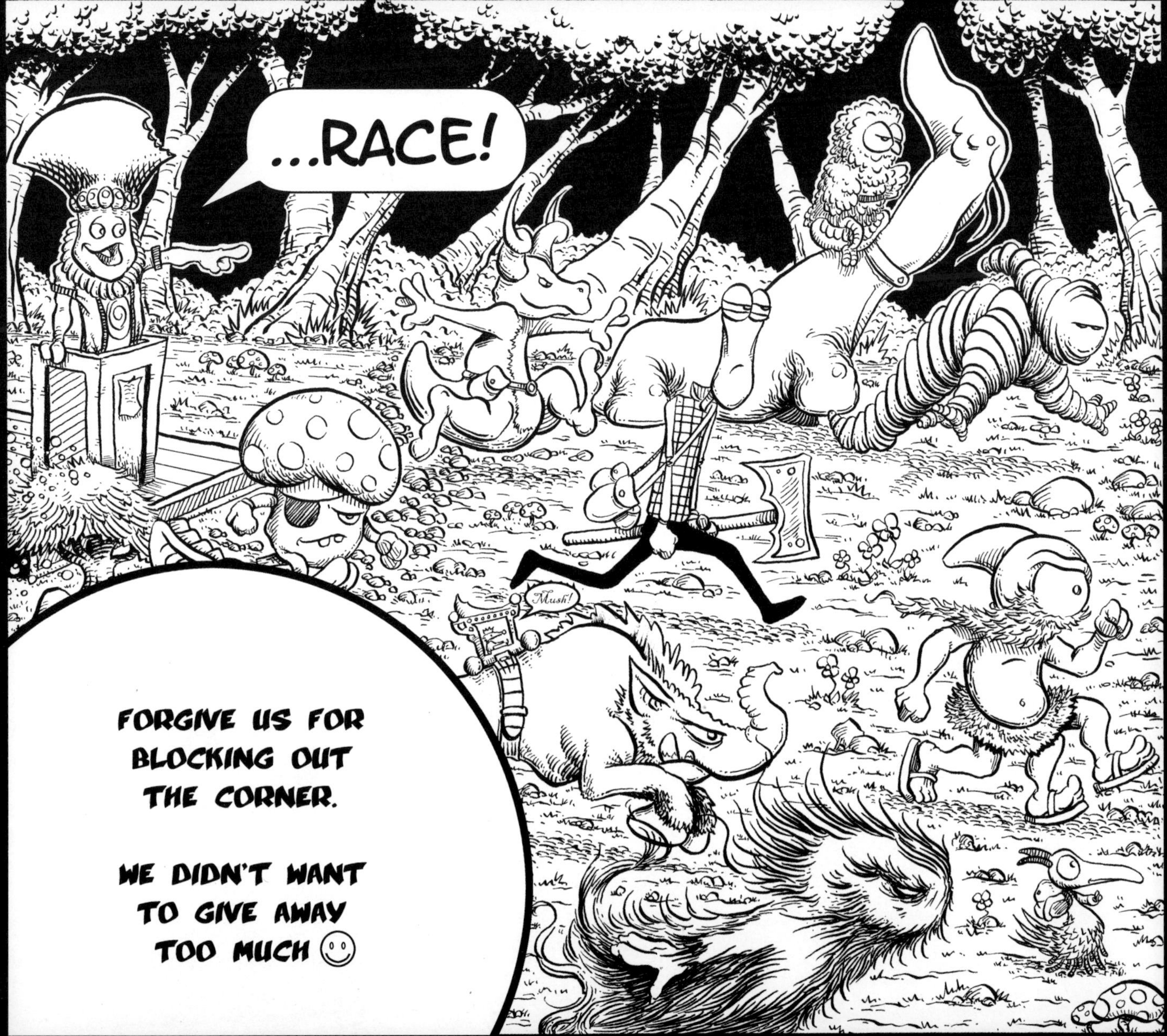
...RACE!
Mush!
FORGIVE US FOR BLOCKING OUT THE CORNER.
WE DIDN'T WANT TO GIVE AWAY TOO MUCH ☺

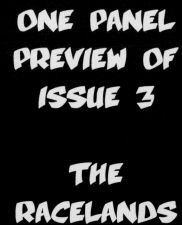

ONE PANEL PREVIEW OF ISSUE 3

THE RACELANDS

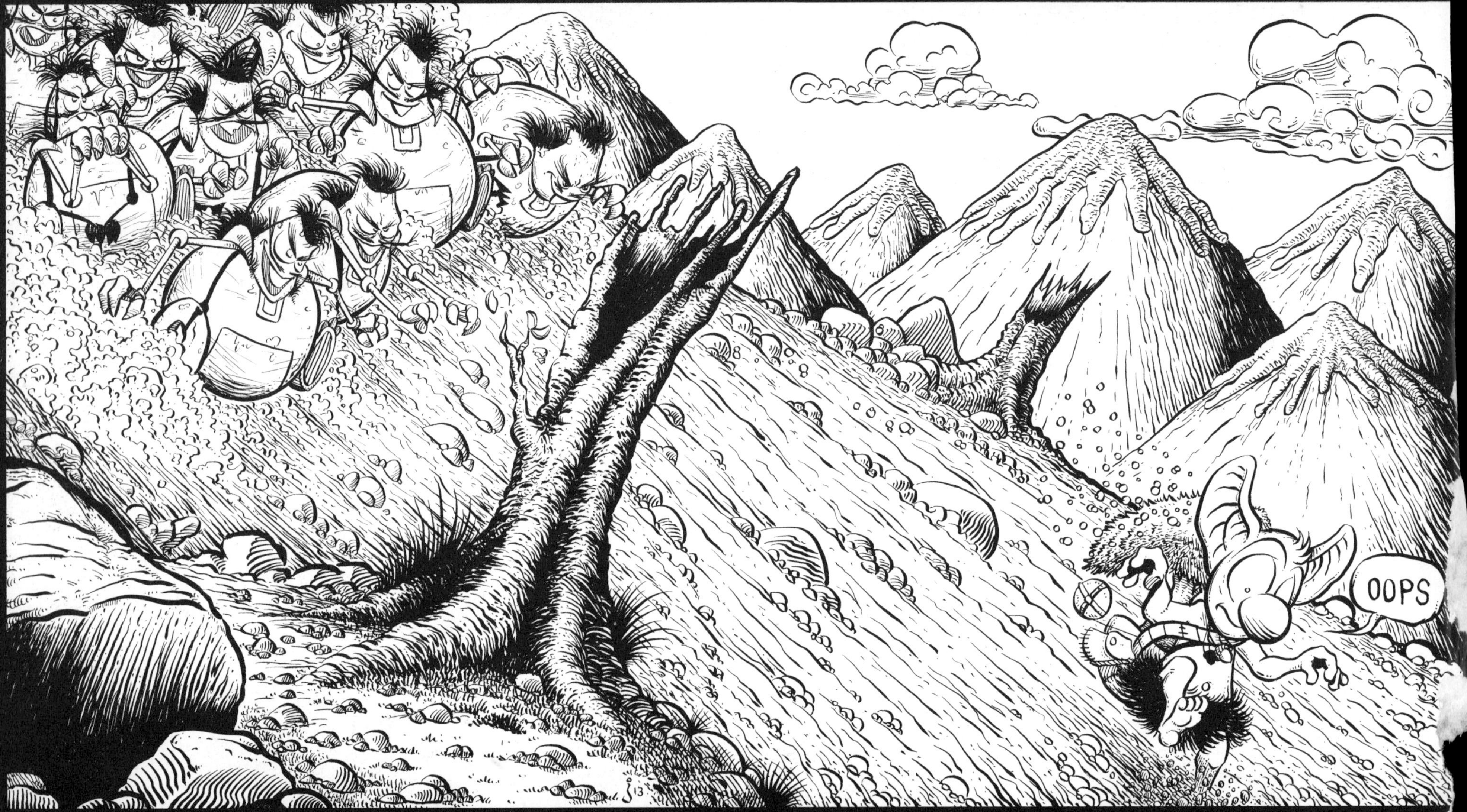
OOPS

COVER #1 - BLACK + WHITE